CIARDI HIMSELF

CIARDI HIMSELF

FIFTEEN ESSAYS IN THE
READING, WRITING, AND
TEACHING OF POETRY

John Ciardi

with a foreword by Edward Cifelli

THE UNIVERSITY OF ARKANSAS PRESS

FAYETTEVILLE · LONDON · 1989

DESIGNER: Chiquita Babb
TYPEFACE: Linotron 202 Goudy Old Style
TYPESETTER: G&S Typesetters, Inc.
PRINTER: Braun-Brumfield, Inc.
BINDER: Braun-Brumfield, Inc.

The paper used in this publication meets the minimum requirements of the
American National Standard for Permanence of Paper for Printed Library
Materials Z39.48-1984. ∞

"The Soul Selects . . ." reprinted by permission of publishers and the Trustees
of Amherst College from *The Poems of Emily Dickinson*, Thomas H. Johnson,
ed., Cambridge, Mass.: The Belknap Press of Harvard University Press, Copyright 1951, © 1955, 1979, 1983 by the President and Fellows of Harvard
College. "The Cancer Cells" from *Collected Poems 1930–1986* by Richard
Eberhart. Copyright © 1960, 1976, 1988 by Richard Eberhart. Reprinted by
permission of Oxford University Press, Inc. "The Traveler's Curse After
Misdirection" from *Poems (1914–26)* by Robert Graves is hereby reprinted by
kind permission of A. P. Watt, Limited, on behalf of the executors of the
estate of Robert Graves.

Frontispiece by Frank Gohlke

LIBRARY OF CONGRESS CATALOGING-IN-PUBLICATION DATA
Ciardi, John, 1916–1986
    Ciardi himself : fifteen essays in the reading, writing, and teaching of
poetry / John Ciardi ; with a foreword by Edward Cifelli.
    p.   cm.
    ISBN 1-55728-084-3 (alk. paper)
    ISBN 1-55728-085-1 (pbk. : alk. paper)
    1. Poetry—History and criticism.   2. Poetry— Authorship.
3. Poetry—Study and teaching. I. Title.
PN688.C53   1989
809.1—dc20   89-31386
                                                          CIP

Contents

FOREWORD

Ciardi the Teacher

J OHN Ciardi was a professor of English at the
University of Kansas City, at Harvard, and at
Rutgers. He was also director of the Bread Loaf Writers Conference in Middlebury, Vermont. He was nationally influential as
poetry editor and columnist for the *Saturday Review*. He wrote a
classic poetry textbook called *How Does a Poem Mean?* And for
three decades he was among the most sought-after speakers on
the college lecture circuit. The point to be made is that even
though we tend to think of John Ciardi more often as a poet and
translator, he spent most of his adult life in classrooms of one sort
or another talking about poetry. And it was very fine talk indeed.

Looking back today at Ciardi's various teaching careers, we
cannot but be impressed at his adaptability, his durability and,
most of all, his courage. For John Ciardi always spoke out on behalf of poets and poetry, sometimes to audiences that had little or
no sense of the poetic art, and at other times to the most aesthet-
ically sophisticated of audiences. And there were times when he
said things that neither audience wanted to hear.

So, for example, in "Twentieth-Century Poetry and Nineteenth-Century Readers," he defends modern poets from readers
whose sense of verse is rooted in the past. Ciardi's message to
readers of poetry is clear: don't expect your poets to be of the
nineteenth century because in order for them to be true, they

ix

must use a language and poetic forms that arise from contemporary America. Nothing else will do.

In "Dear N:" Ciardi addresses a friend who has sent him a poem about the emotions he felt on becoming a parent for the first time. But the poem is a poor one, and Ciardi feels himself tugged in opposite directions by the claims of friendship and poetry. At first he tries to explain the poetic problems, but finds himself impatient at last: "I'll risk your dislike if I can make you see you have squandered good feeling on language that isn't good enough for what you are feeling." Ciardi would be as gentle as possible with the world at large, but honesty always won out. Sometimes it was a painful honesty.

In "The Student Poet," Ciardi makes points useful for any student poet, whether in a beginner's creative writing course at college or at the Bread Loaf Writers Conference. His messages usually return to the theme of technical mastery, to revision and discipline and craftsmanship, and so they do here: "In the arts the student will do better only as he is willing to accept the difficulty of working within fixed disciplines. In poetry the fixed disciplines are rhyme, metrics, and form." While these points will sound eminently sensible to many, today as in past years, some—students and established poets alike—will see Ciardi's views as old-fashioned and Ciardi himself autocratic in their defense. I think it still does him honor to say in the face of such criticism that "an accomplished writer may venture into free verse when he is sufficiently sure of himself, but no student can permit himself such assurance."

I suggest that such boldness of expression is the joy of John Ciardi as essayist and teacher. Throughout his work on poetry, here as elsewhere, we encounter the measured language of his formal challenges to poets, teachers, and students. Ciardi leads us in these fifteen essays very deliberately to a better sense of what the poet ought to be doing, what the reader of poetry ought to be looking for, and what the teacher of poetry ought to be trying for in the classroom—all the sort of thing that enabled John Ciardi to emerge as his generation's most forceful, entertaining, and principled spokesman for the craft of poetry.

But the joy of John Ciardi is greater than the boldness of his statements. He is also a master sentence- and phrase-maker. Consider these, from the pages of this book:

I have learned not to send a poem on a prose errand.

The craft [of poetry] is not easy. It is better than easy. It is joyously difficult.

Language haunts the writer. Words, sentences, rhythms are not things to the writer; they are presences.

The bad writer is easily self-persuaded to take the power of the starting emotion as a measure of the writing.

It is never the size of a thing looked at that counts but the size of the mind that is doing the looking.

I would rather be confused by Shakespeare than clarified by my broker.

For those who have encountered John Ciardi elsewhere, perhaps in the *Saturday Review* or in *How Does a Poem Mean?* or in one of his coast-to-coast lectures on poetry, some of these lines will sound familiar; yet even in repetition they have the right mix of axiomatic memorability and good common sense.

When we think of John Ciardi as teacher, then, we think first of an essayist and lecturer with courage enough to speak in defense of the disciplined management of poetic form. But we undoubtedly think of him also as a verbal virtuoso, a prose master who seems to mark every lesson with memorable lines.

Ciardi Himself is an excellent introduction to the man and his thoughts on the painstaking craftsmanship involved in the art of writing poetry. There are hard lessons here, but in the hands of this master teacher, it's easy going.

Edward Cifelli

CIARDI HIMSELF

The Act of Language

A<small>T</small> the beginning of *The Divine Comedy*, Dante finds himself in a Dark Wood, lost from the light of God.

As soon as he realizes that he is in darkness, he looks up and sees the first light of the dawn shawling the shoulders of a little hill. (In Dante, the Sun is always a symbol of God as Divine Illumination.) The allegory should be clear enough: the very realization that one is lost is the beginning of finding oneself.

What happens next is the heart of the matter. His goal in sight, Dante tries to race straight up the hill to reach the light by direct assault. Almost immediately his way is blocked by three beasts—a Leopard, a Lion, and a She-wolf—representing all the sins of the world.

The beasts drive Dante back into the darkness. There he comes on the soul of Virgil, who symbolizes Human Reason. Virgil explains that a man may reach the light only by going the long way round. Dante must risk the dangerous

3

descent into Hell and he must make the arduous ascent of Purgatory. Only then may he enter, bit by bit, the final presence of the light, which is to say Heaven.

The point of the parable is that in art as in theology—as in all things that concern people in their profoundest moments—the long way round is the only way home. Shortcuts are useful only in mechanics. One who seeks mortal understanding must go the long way.

The poet's way round is through rhythm, diction, image, and form. It is the right, the duty, and the joy of his trade to be passionate about these things, in the minutest and even the most frivolous detail. To be passionate about them, if need be, to the exclusion of what is generally understood by "sincerity" and "meaning." To be more passionate about them than he is about the cold war, the Gunpowder Plot, the next election, abolition, the H-bomb, the Inquisition, juvenile delinquency, the Spanish Armada, or his own survival.

Good poets have not generally sneered at the world of affairs. Some have, but many others have functioned well within it. Yet the need and the right of all poets to detach themselves from the things of the world in order to pursue the things of the poetic trade have always been inseparable from their success as poets.

The poet must be passionate about the four elements of his trade—rhythm, diction, image, and form—for the most fundamental of reasons. He must be so because those passions are both a joy and an addiction within him. Because they are the life of the poem, without which nothing of value can happen either in the poem or to the reader. Because a poem cannot be written well except as these passions inform it.

Because it is an act of language, a good poem is deeply connected with everything we are and do. For language is one of the most fundamental activities in which human beings engage. Take away language, and you take away most of our ability to think and to experience. Enrich language, and you cannot fail to enrich our experience. Whenever we have let great language into our heads, we have been richer for it.

But we are not made richer by what is being said. It is the language itself that brings enrichment. Could poetry be meaningful aside from its act of language, it would have no reason for being, and the whole history of poetry could be reduced to a series of simple paraphrases.

The office (or the aesthetic norm) in charge of letting assumptions loose in the land seems to have decreed (largely, I suspect, with the aid of the school system) that a poem is a way of dealing with something called a "subject"; that relentless paraphrase can identify that subject and, in so doing, render a poem "understandable"; and that the "importance" or "magnitude" of the poem is directly determined by the importance and magnitude of the subject.

Yeats once quoted John Dunsany's agitation following a performance in which an actor had read some of Dunsany's poetry. "I took a devil of a lot of trouble," Dunsany exclaimed, "to make poetry of it, and that fellow read it as if it were prose!" It seems safe to assume "that fellow" had read all the words of the poems, whereby the subject, if any, had been stated. Once again, then, it seems fair to assume that Dunsany's ire was stirred by his concern for something that was not the subject. At a guess, he was offended by the failure to render his tones, cadences, pauses, and rhythmic balances and counterbalances.

The general assumption that a poem is a way of dealing with a subject must be tested against the fact that poets seem to care a great deal about something else the poem does. As a possible useful simplification, that "something else" can be divided into diction, image or metaphor, rhythm, and form.

5

When Henry Rago in a poem titled, as I recall, "The Coming on of Twilight in a Village in Haiti," wrote, "The waves were all one rosy influence," he was taking a poet's delight in his own word choice. An "influence," in the derived sense of the word, is "that which has a power to affect." At root, influence means "a flowing in." The poet has, in effect, punned on the (Latin) *influens*, the flowing in of the waves (which are made rosy by the sunset). They flow in upon him in the root sense and they influence his mood in the derived sense. How sweetly the word, in this context of sunset waves, chimes its first meaning against its new meaning. A damnation on all who must repeat the old saw that a pun is the lowest form of humor. This kind of pun can be the sweet excellence of a choice poetic diction. Certainly Rago must have been filled with pleasure at the rightness of his own choice in much the way a musician must quicken to pleasure at the achievement of perfect tone. I confess I have forgotten what the rest of Rago's poem was "about"—if it was about anything. It is that one word choice that remains unforgettable as an instant of achieved poetry.

Can that pleasure be made to register on the insistently literal, who want to see that Beethoven's "di-di-di-DAH" is explainable as "fate knocking on the door"?

To reduce the language of the arts to such baby food metaphors is to take the artist's adulthood away. Di-di-di-DAH came into Beethoven's mind not as a classroom paraphrase, but as a musical idea. It awakened in him, I will guess, no impulse to statement but a sense of excited possibility. It is that sense we must guess at, but to guess we must first remember that Beethoven, not only by genius but by an intense training, was better equipped than we are to be excited by a musical idea. He had mastered orchestration, symphonic tradition and form, counterpoint, theory, and a sense of his own idiom—mastered them to the point at which the intricacies of form and technique (that most of us would have to spell out laboriously, one detail at a time) came to him not as an examination to be taken and passed, but as a feeling.

Had he been forced to analyze that feeling, he might perhaps have stammered something to the effect that di-di-di-DAH sounded firmly portentous as an opening, that it suggested a rhythmic pattern that would weave well into whatever followed, that it would transpose well from instrument to instrument, that it seemed both simple and capable of subtle involvement. He might even have added that he had started with other musical ideas that had given him a similar sense of excited possibility and had petered out, but that he wanted to explore this one to see what came of it.

Something much like that, in something like the same context, will do for the poet's way of receiving poetic ideas. An aesthetic idea is not a logical process. It is to some extent a happenstance. It comes in perhaps the way a Pacific Island once came to the early explorers. Some must have seemed barren wastes at a glance. Others must have seemed enticing. If his situation had left him free to ignore what seemed barren and to land on what seemed alluring, the mariner then had an island to explore. He did not know what island it would be; he would learn that as he went.

The difference between the explorer of islands and the explorer of aesthetic ideas is that the mariner maps the island he finds there, while the artist's islands are invented by the artist.

In each case, though—the composer hearing a musical idea, the mariner sighting an island, the poet undertaking a theme—it is better to think of the starting impulse not as a subject but as that sense of excitement that can be felt by a person with a lifelong practice at responding to such possibilities. And, let it be hoped, with a talent for them.

~ If there is in fact a subject to a poem, it may quite con-

ceivably be found by the poet after the poem is written.
The past few decades we have seen a lot of "concrete"
poetry. Consider an abstract example by—was it Eugene
Jolas?—from the twenties. The poem is simply an arrangement of the twenty-six letters of the alphabet. I am not sure
I remember how Jolas grouped his letters or what he called
the poem. I don't think it matters much; let's assume he
grouped them so:

ABCDE

FGHIJ

KLMNO

PQRST

UVWXY

Z

And let us assume he then called it "Monday" or "By the
Atlantic" or "Love." Could the titles reach for a subject
matter to whatever shape his poetic idea had spoken? In
whatever case, the shape would be primary and the subject
an afterthought.

It might go a bit further. Once I have seen his idea, I
might decide to work it closer to a possible subject. I will
reshape it so:

AB

CDE

FGH

I!

JK

LMN

O!

PQ

RST

U!

8

    V W
    X!
    Y?—Z.

I am, of course, punning through the alphabet and I decide
to call my pun "Suicide." This suicide runs through a series
of irrelevant letters punctuated by "I" and an exclamation
point: the assertion of one-ness. There follow more letters
and then "O!" I am, of course, punning on "Oh!" My next
pun is on "You!" My next on "Ex!" My next on "Why?"
the answer to which is "Z," the Omega of the life series.
But I might as readily have turned my (not very good) trick
in another direction by calling it "On Being Through with
Salty-Low, or Bye-Bye Baby, It's Time to Take a Nap." In
that case, I think I might be tempted to use question marks
instead of exclamation points after the selected letters on
which I pun. "I?" would then, I hope, pun on "Who me?"
"O?" would pun on "Oh, you don't say?" "U?" would pun
on "You?" as in "Who?—You?" "X?" would remain the
same pun but in a different context. And, to show my su-
preme indifference (and to get back to the "nap" planted in
my subtitle), I might end with

    Y?—Zzzzz.

to indicate that I find the matter not tragic but only
soporific.

No matter how I retitle, shift the arrangement, or rework
the puns, it is the trick that matters. The subject, if any, is
there to stage the game in, and if need be, I will alter the
stage to my pleasure so long as the game may be served.

This alphabetical example is, of course, almost pure
abstraction. To get closer to where we live, consider as
simple a passage as the beginning of Herrick's "Upon Julia's
Clothes":

9

Whenas in silks my Julia goes,
Then, then, methinks, how sweetly flows
The liquefaction of her clothes.

Who can read those lines without a thrill of pleasure? But now consider the paraphrase: "I like the rustle of Julia's silks when she walks." The poetry and the paraphrase are about equal in subject matter. The difference is that the poetry is a full and rich act of language, whereas the paraphrase lacks, among other things, measure, pause, stress, rhyme, and the pleasure of lingering over the word "liquefaction."

"But what is Julia doing there?" cries that voice of common sense. "She must have something to do with the poem or she wouldn't be in it!"

The owner of that voice would do well to ponder the relation between a good portrait and its subject. The subject is there, to be sure—at least in most cases. But the instant the painter puts one brush stroke on the canvas and then another, the two brush strokes take on a relation to each other and to the space around them. The two then take on a relation to the third, and it to them. And so forth. The painting immediately begins to exert its own demands upon the painter, its own way of going. Immediately the subject begins to disappear.

All too soon, for that matter, the subject will have changed with age or will have died. After a while, no living person will have any recollection of what the subject looked like. All that will remain then is a portrait head, which must be either self-validating or worthless. Because the subject cannot validate the painting, he or she will have become irrelevant. All that can finally validate the portrait is the way in which the painter engaged the act of painting.

And one more thing—the good artist always thinks in long terms, and knows, even at the moment of the painting, that both painter and subject will disappear. Any good painter will be painting for the painting and for the time when the subject will have blown away into time.

So with poetry. The one final and enduring meaning of any poem lies not in what it seems to have set out to say, but in its act of language.

The only test of the act of language is the memory of the race. Bad poetry is by nature forgettable; it is, therefore, soon forgotten. Good poetry, like any good act of language, hooks onto human memory and stays there. Write well, and there will always be someone somewhere who carries in mind what you have written. It will stay in memory because man is the language animal, and because his need of language is from the roots of his consciousness. That need in him is not a need for meaning. Rather, good language in him takes possession of meaning; it fills him with a resonance that the best of us understand only dimly, but without which no one is entirely alive. Poetry is that presence and that resonance. As Archibald MacLeish put it in his much-discussed "Ars Poetica":

> A poem should not mean
> But be.

I began teaching at what was then the University of Kansas City before the war, in 1940, and I had a number of enthusiastic bachelor researches to undertake. One of them was a girl in Chicago, and one was a girl in Kansas City. I seemed to spend a lot of time on the Streamliners, going back and forth from one to the other. My salary just about kept the Atchison, Topeka, and Santa Fe rolling, as nearly as I can recall. I would find myself in the smoker with this world's traveling salesmen. They met there. They would begin a ritual. It always seemed to have the same opening phrase. They would say, "What are you *in?*"

This man would say he was in glue, and they would talk about that for a while.

Then they would say, "What are *you* in?"

This man would say he was in brass doorknobs, and they would talk about brass doorknobs for a while.

Then they would turn to me and say, "What are *you* in?"

At first I used to invent things. I had a feeling that it would take too much explanation to tell a bar car full of salesmen that I was a poet. It's a little like wearing neckties. I think they are silly. Every once in a while, in an excess of character, I would go to school in the morning without a necktie and spend the rest of the day explaining how come I had forgotten my necktie. So the next day I would wear it. It's easier to conform than to defend character, if you are going to get any work done.

But one day, for the fun of it, when the question came to me, "What are *you* in?" I said, "I'm a poet." It took very little explanation. As a matter of fact, there was a long silence, in which people detached and regrouped. After a suitable interval, I went into the main body of the car and sat down. Then I began to discover—I had begun doing this brazenly and experimentally—that not every time, but frequently, a salesman would slide into the seat next to mine and begin talking in a low voice. He had something that he wanted to say to me that he could not say to other salesmen. Or maybe, since I was so obviously shameless, he could confess all to me. But often he would have a poem in his wallet.

Every one of them would make the terrifying mistake that all bad poets and all overenthusiastic people make— the assumption that if the subject is large enough, it does not matter whether or not the poem is good. If you can just take the largest possible subject and begin with "Truth is . . . ," "Beauty is . . . ," "Life is . . . ," you've got to end up beautiful. Unfortunately for these very intense and soulful creatures, the size of the poem is not determined by the size of the subject. It is determined by the size of the mind that is trying to address the subject. It is a very different thing. The value of a science is not decided by the value of the subject it studies. Otherwise microbiologists would be insignificant people and only geologists would really count.

I had a lovely exchange at the *Saturday Review* with a woman whose poems I had rejected. I got about 500 a week, and could accept only two. But she took this personally, as many do, and wrote me a hot letter. I had not remembered the poems, but she said, in a very ladylike way, "I suppose you rejected my poem because it was about God."

I usually did not answer my mail. But I could not resist the snarl in her assumption. "Dear Madam:" I wrote, "I did not reject your poem because it was about God. I rejected it because I could not conquer a feeling that you were not equal to the subject."

An oration is not a poem. A poem is a living performance. Great human feeling will make nothing out of the cello until the fingering arm and the bowing arm have gone to school. It takes at least as much discipline to write a poem as it does to play the cello well. The feeling is there, yes, but communication of feeling is a skill—a way of doing. It involves pain; it involves difficulty. Robert Frost spoke of "the pleasure of taking pains." That is the aesthetic joy.

I have never seen a child, however small, who did not get some joy out of playing patty-cake. I am going to conclude from that that babies are born with a poetic impulse. When they are playing patty-cake, they are forming language, they are keeping a meter, they are keeping a rhyme going, and they are doing something with their bodies. Perhaps I am misreading the surface clues, but it seems to me this is a natural human joy, trying to get back into this rhythmic pace.

As my own children grew older, I began to write poems for them. In the course of writing those poems, I found myself visiting some lower grades, and I discovered that one of the most joyous and natural and perfect audiences for poetry in this world is a class of bright third-graders. Nothing matches it. Everything is immediate, real, alive, without inhibitions, all out-flowing identification and joy. Any life, I think, has to start in joy, that appetite for life, that walking out to find such a day as you find. It is here for pleasure.

But now and then I have gone to high schools to talk about poetry. Oh, and they are dead! I don't know who delivered the deathblow. I don't know how it came around. But somewhere between the third and the eleventh grade, something important, a potential source of joy and rejoicing, has died. I find myself wanting to ask some questions about it, because I think it concerns all of us. Why is it that every American child delivered to the school system starts as a natural audience for poetry and almost every child who leaves it hates the stuff? I think he perhaps has been "Evangelized," if that is one of the poems that did it through the teaching method.

I sometimes think children should not happen to adults; they should just happen to other children. No adult has the energy to keep up with them. It is a kind of race one is constantly and despairingly losing all the way through life. But, whatever else, the child has a natural, violent, overflowing, joyous imagination. The healthy child always knows the difference between "for real" violence and "pretend" violence. They go "Bang! Bang! You're dead!" and they want you to fall on the floor. But there is no thought in this of firing real bullets. It is a projection of emotional dramas going on inside the child. So I began to write poems I felt spoke to my childhood and to my children's childhood.

Children take poems for their sounds and images, not for their messages. You can destroy a poem by message-hunting it. I love a sentence I picked up in a very unlikely place, in

14

a science fiction story. It said, satirizing a would-be poet, "He sold his birthright for a pot of message."

My good friend David McCord had a poem I have always cherished.

> Big Chief Watapotami
> Sat in the sun and said, "Me hot am I."
> Sat in the shade and said, "Me cooler."
> Such is the life of an Indian ruler.

Now, "In two good sentences that make sense, state the meaning of that poem." There is none.

Another piece of light verse that I think makes this point extremely well is one by Margaret Fishback.

> O Somewhere there are people who
> Have nothing in the world to do
> But sit upon the Pyrenees
> And use the very special breeze
> Provided for the people who
> Have nothing in the world to do . . .

You can go for as long as you like. You see, that is not about the Pyrenees. The Pyrenees are in there to rhyme with breeze, and breeze is in there to rhyme with Pyrenees, and this whole thing is an exercise in self-delighting form. Now if it has self-delighting form, it can then go on to say something.

I think we will all agree that some of the master perceptions, that some of the most ringing and resonant, enduring statements made about the human condition on this planet have been made by the poets. But they have been made only and always by those poets who kept their whole joy in picking the words because they match one another, in finding the rhythms that flow, in the joy in metaphor, and the joy in form.

I am trying to say that the music of this world is played by musicians who love their instruments, and the instruments of poetry are diction, image or metaphor, rhythm, and form; and to throw all of that out for categorical discussions on the history of ideas, I think, is to lose too much. I am not against the study of the history of ideas, except that is a history course; it is not a course in poetry. It is literary history, to be sure, but I think our attention should be to what makes a poem, if we want to write or read poetry.

Let me offer a perhaps frivolous poem—one I have always liked—to show what I think are some of the human benefits of rhythm, because, as you have discovered by now, I am only lightly serious and obviously seriously light. I don't know how to separate the two from each other. But I think it is a happy balance.

Here is a poem by Robert Graves, "The Traveler's Curse After Misdirection." It's from the Welsh. Obviously a man has been sent in all sorts of directions all day long. At the end of his weary day, he is completely lost and thinks back to the people who directed him, and he has some sentiments to express, as you might say. May I point out that though he starts in anger, he picks up such a lovely rhythm that he has to end in joy. This is one of the ways of forgiving your enemies. If you can begin denouncing them in so happy a rhythm that you end up joyous, you are prepared for mercy and forgiveness.

> May they wander stage by stage
> Of the same vain pilgrimage,
> Stumbling on, age after age,
> Night and day, mile after mile,
> At each and every step, a stile;
> At each and every stile, withal,
> May they catch their feet and fall;
> At each and every fall they take,

May a bone within them break;
And may the bones that break within
Not be, for variation's sake,
Now rib, now thigh, now arm, now shin,
But always, without fail, THE NECK.

I submit to you that the man had to end up happy. But isn't that in the nature of a rhythm, to start with any feeling and then lift it—isn't that by nature the same pleasure refined and elevated that we get in the magnificent rhythm of, for example,

From the round earth's imagined corners
Blow your trumpets, angels, and arise,
Arise ye numberless infinities of souls. . . .

That is language being enlarged by rhythm.

Our central method of knowledge is our language. I do not think it is the function of the poets to give us homilies with it, but to try to work the language to the limits of its resources, because when it is so worked, it has to be humanizing; it has to be a way of knowledge, because it is as deep inside ourselves as any part of our being.

Like the great rhythms. Here is the opening stanza of John Donne's "The Anniversarie":

All kings, and all their favorites,
All glory of honors, beauties, wits,
The Sun it selfe, which makes times as they passe,
Is elder by a yeare, now, than it was
When thou and I first one another saw:
All other things, to their destruction draw,
Only our love hath no decay:
This, no to morrow hath, nor yesterday.
Running, it never runs from us away,
But truly keeps his first, last, everlasting day.

Worldly things pass away, but true love is constant, says the subject matter. All true enough, and tried enough. But listen to the rhythm enforce itself upon the saying, especially in the last four lines. For present purposes, let the voice ignore the lesser accents. Let it stress only those syllables printed in capital letters below, while observing the pauses as indicated by the slash marks. And forget the meaning. Read for the emphasis and the pauses:

> Only OUR LOVE hath no deCAY//
> THIS//no to MOrrow hath// nor YESterday//
> RUNning// it never runs from us aWAY//
> But truly keeps his FIRST//LAST//EVerlasting DAY

Not all rhythms are so percussive, so measured out by pauses, and so metrically irregular. Listen to this smoother rhythm from Poe's "Israfel":

> If I could dwell
> Where Israfel
>   Hath dwelt, and he where I,
> He might not sing so wildly well
>   A mortal melody,
> While a bolder note than his might swell
>   From my lyre within the sky.

Or rhythm may be very percussive, but without substantial pauses, as in the last line of this passage from the end of Gerard Manley Hopkins' "Felix Randal," an elegy for a blacksmith:

> How far from then forethought of, all thy more
>   boisterous years,
> When thou at the random grim forge, powerful
>   amidst peers,
> Didst fettle for the great gray drayhorse his bright
>   and battering sandal.

Listen to the hammerfall of that last line: "Didst FEttle for the GREAT GRAY DRAYhorse his BRIGHT and BAttering SANdal."

Or listen to the spacing of the "ah" sounds as a rhythmic emphasis in the last line of this final passage from Meredith's "Lucifer in Starlight":

> Around the ancient track marched, rank on rank,
> The ARmy of unALterable LAW.

Percussive, smooth, flowing, or studded with pauses— there is no end to the variety and delight of great language rhythms. For the poet, his rhythms are forever more than a matter of making a "meaningful" statement; they are a joy in their own right. No poet hates meaning. But the poet's passion is for the triumph of language. No reader can come to real contact with a poem except through the joy of that rhythmic act of language.

As for the rhythm, so for diction. The poet goes to language—or it comes to him and he receives it—for his joy in the precision of great word choices. Give him such a line as Whitman's "I witness the corpse with the dabbled hair," and he will register the corpse, to be sure, but it will be "dabbled" he seizes upon with the joy of a botanist coming on a rare specimen. So when Keats speaks of Ruth amid "the alien corn" or when Theodore Roethke speaks of sheep "strewn" on a field, the good reader will certainly care about the dramatic situation of the poem, but cannot fail to answer with a special joy to "alien" and to "strewn."

What, after all, is the subject as compared to the joy in such rich precision? Thousands of English poems have described the passing of winter and the coming of spring. Certainly there is little in that subject as a subject to attract us. But listen to the pure flutefall of the word choices I have italicized in the following passage from Stanley Kunitz's

"Deciduous Bough," and note how the delight in language makes everything immediate and new again:

> Winter that *coils* in the thicket now
> Will *glide* from the field, the *swinging* rain
> Be *knotted* with flowers, on every bough
> A bird will *meditate* again.

"Poetry," said Coleridge, "is the best words in the best order." How can anyone reading the Kunitz passage escape a sense that the language is being diligently selected? The delight one feels in coming on such language is not only in the experience of perfection but also in the fact that perfection has been made to seem not only effortless but inevitable.

And let this much more be added to the idea of poetic meaning: nothing in a good poem happens by accident; every word, every comma, every variant spelling must enter as an act of the poet's choice. A poem is a machine for making choices. The mark of the good poet is the refusal to make easy or cheap choices. The better the poet, the greater the demands he makes upon himself, and the higher he sets his level of choice. Thus, a good poem is not only an act of mind but an act of devotion to mind. The poet who chooses cheaply or lazily is guilty of aesthetic acedia, and he is lost thereby. The poet who spares nothing in his search for the most demanding choices is shaping a human attention that offers itself as a high—and joyful—example to all readers of mind and devotion. Every act of great language, whatever its subject matter, illustrates an idea of order and a resonance of human possibility without which no mind can sense its own fullest dimensions.

As for rhythm and diction, so for imagery. To be sure, every word is at root an image, and poetic images must be made of words. Yet certainly there is in a well-constructed image an effect that cannot be said to rise from any one word choice, but from the total phrasing.

So for the sensory shiver of Keats' "The silver snarling trumpets 'gan to chide." So for the wonderfully woozy effect of John Frederick Nims' "The drunk clambering on his undulant floor." So for the grand hyperbole of Howard Nemerov saying that the way a young girl looks at him "sets his knees to splashing like two waves."

We learn both imagination and precision from the poet's eye. And we learn correspondences. Consider the following image from "Areopagus" by Louis MacNeice, a poem as playful as it is serious, in which MacNeice describes Athens as a cradle of the Western mind. Cradles, he makes clear, generally contain children, and all those boy-gods and girl-goddesses had their childish side:

> . . . you still may glimpse
> The child-eyed Fury tossing her shock of snakes,
> Careering over the Parthenon's ruined playpen.

It is a bit shocking to have the Parthenon spoken of as a playpen, but once the shock has passed, what a triumph there is in the figure: everything corresponds! Think how much would have been lost had the Parthenon a surviving roof, or had its general proportions or the placement of the pillars' slats resisted the comparison. The joy of it is that, despite the first shock, nothing resists the comparison; and we find that the surprise turns out to be a true correspondence.

One of the poet's happiest—and most mortal—games is in seeking such correspondences. But what flows from them is more than a game. Every discovery of true correspondence is an act of reason and an instruction to the mind. For intelligence does not consist of masses of factual detail. It consists of seeing essential likenesses and essential differences and of relating them, allowing for differences within the likenesses and for likenesses within the differences. Mentality is born of analogy.

Note, too, that the image-idea of "ruined playpen" does not simply happen but is prepared for in "child-eyed." And note, further, the nice double meaning of "careering" as both a wild rush and to make a career of.

A good extended image, that is to say, is made of various elements and is marked by both sequence and structure. Thus we have already touched upon the essence of the fourth element of the poet's trade: form.

There are many kinds of poetic form, but since all are based on pattern and sequence, let a tightly patterned poem illustrate. Here is Emily Dickinson's "The Soul Selects":

> The Soul selects her own Society—
> Then—shuts the Door—
> To her divine Majority—
> Present no more—
>
> Unmoved—she notes the Chariots—pausing—
> At her low Gate—
> Unmoved—an Emperor be kneeling
> Upon her Mat—
>
> I've known her—from an ample nation—
> Choose One—
> Then—close the Valves of her attention—
> Like Stone—

Whatever the hunters of beauty and truth find for their pleasure in such a poem, the poet's joy will be in its form and management. He responds to the passion of the language for its own sparseness, to the pattern of rhyme and half-rhyme, to the flavor of the images (connotation), and to the way those flavors relate to one another. He responds to the interplay of the four-foot feminine lines (which end on an unaccented syllable) and the two-foot masculine lines (which end on an accented syllable).

And he responds, above all, to the way those two-foot lines develop in the last stanza into two boldly-stroked syllables apiece (monosyllabic feet) so that the emotion held down throughout the poem by the sparseness of the language is hammered into sensation by the beat of those last two words: "Like Stone"—thud! thud!

Beauty and truth are no irrelevancies, but they are abstractions that must remain meaningless to poetry until they are brought to being in the management of a specific form. It is that management the poet must love: the joy of sensing that the poem falls into an inescapable form, and therefore into an inescapable experience. For the poet's trade is not to talk about experience, but to make it happen. The act of making is all a poet knows of beauty and truth. It is, in fact, the way of knowing them.

As I. A. Richards, poet and scholar of the language, put it in a poem titled "The Ruins":

> Sometimes a word is wiser much than men:
> "Faithful" e.g., "responsible" and "true."
> And words it is, not poets, make up poems.
> Our words, we say, but we are theirs, too,
> For words made men and may unmake again.

The act of the poem is its act of language. That act is the true final subject and meaning of any poem. It is to that act of language the poet shapes his most devoted attention—to the fullness of rhythm, diction, image or metaphor, and form. Only in that devotion can a poet seize the world and make it evident.

The Rage for Honesty

WHY POETRY CHANGES

THERE can be no dishonest reason for writing a poem. What is written badly is written helplessly by honest wish that lacks talent. Poetry, as Eliot put it, is written against "the general mess of imprecision of feeling." A good poem is emotionally precise. Emily Dickinson, in sending her poems to Higginson, kept asking "Have I said It true?"

Nor do poets walk away from the admired masters of their childhood, in an act of scorn. Wordsworth at his best is a considerable poet. It is possible and a due respect to admire his best today. It is not possible for a good poet to write in his manner. To reject that manner as a possible model for one's own is no act of contempt, but only an assertion of honesty. His language seems artificial unless the reader makes an historic allowance. As much could be said of his themes and of the tacked-on morals with which he brings them to a sermon close. But, above all, Wordsworth believed in purity of motives.

25

Now suppose I were to write a poem in the manner of Wordsworth's "The Leech Gatherers," or in the manner of the Lucy poems. Coming to the end, how could I fail to feel uneasy? Asking "Have I said it true?", I must doubt that I have. I must doubt that anything is that simple. "True" for us, in these days, in the sense of precision of feeling, must mean "in exactly balanced ambiguity."

But I cannot hope to achieve even that exactly balanced ambiguity in the rhetoric of the dust, nor can I come to such thumping resolutions as:

> Where every prospect pleases
> And only man is vile.

It is a strictly limited landscape in which every prospect pleases, and though man can be vile, he is also something else. If I am to write honestly, I must be wary of simplified high-mindedness, of rhetorical overstatements, and of final assertions.

There were interim periods. Emily Dickinson and Gerard Manley Hopkins were writing in seclusion and writing in new and enduring voices. Baudelaire was transmitting powerful influences to a few English poets. Whitman was roaring his artful liberation from the stricture of pattern.

The poetic revolution of this century happened between 1910 and 1925. Yeats, starting as a limpwrist romantic, created a powerful poetry out of speech, a percussive metric, and a complicated symbolism. Frost (he appeared late, but most of his poems had been written by 1910 to be shed out in small volumes for many years) attuned the cadences of American speech to a metric of his own. Pound and Eliot crossbred English poetry to the poetry of the world. Wallace Stevens, deeply enamored of French poetry, found a new genre, not exactly an abstract poetry, but one that moved on its own assertions as if the world were real only because he willed its parts into imagination. E. E. Cummings, Archibald MacLeish, and Marianne Moore formed voices unlike any that had been heard before, difficult at times, but always emotionally precise. And William Carlos Williams, indefatigable and self-effacing, went on year after year making a master body of poetry whose motto was "no ideas but in things."

There were, of course, the lesser experimentalists, but these poets were the masters and schoolmasters of the age and still remain so. Only W. H. Auden, a late arrival, can stand beside them. Theodore Roethke might have been one of them, I think, but he was born too late for the revolution.

It was a revolution of sensibility. Stephen Crane was a forerunner. F. S. Flint had a minor influence on *vers libres,* which should not be translated as "free verse" but as liberated verse, verse freed of tired rhyme and rhetoric and metric, and of moral assertion. It was Ezra Pound, though, who took over the movement, or thought he did. Amy Lowell did her best to snatch it from him, converting "imagism" to "Amygism." In retrospect, however, it is William Carlos Williams who emerges as the master imagist.

Pound, nevertheless, was the master teacher if not the master maker. He was domineering, he craved the authority of a literary czar, yet he was an obsessive reader and an acute identifier of talent. He, more than any other, taught the age its poetic techniques. If he does not himself emerge as a master poet, he was the master shaper of poetic sensibilities.

It was not his eccentricity that made him so pervasive a force. Pound had an infallible eye for the emotional precision of poetry. If he was often intemperate in his scorn of the "would-be-better-than-life" poets, his was still a rage for honesty.

It is the rage for honesty that brings us back to the source of poetic change. Even these master poets must, at times, have found themselves writing in the rhetorical manner of the nineteenth century, reaching for purple flourishes, raising their voices in the hope of achieving an ecstasy. In the persuasion of midnight and in the enchantment of one's own words, any poet can write badly. Come then the cold morning light of revision, and one knows he has lied, that he cannot write in the old way and still say it true to his own feelings.

Let me dare say, as a possibly terrifying oversimplification, that there is no more than that to poetic change. If the poet must reject an old way of writing as untrue to his feelings, he must either stop writing or find a new way.

Nor does it matter that many others will continue to write as if there had been no necessary change in aesthetic sensibility since Wordsworth. "Mankind cannot stand very much reality," sighed Eliot. "Strike through the mist," cried Melville. It took a new poetry, the poetry of a sensibility shocked by World War I, to catch the cadences, the ambivalences, and the imagery of our lives.

The poetry of that new sensibility had already found its means when the old *Saturday Review of Literature* was founded in 1924. *SRL* was not receptive to the change. Among the movers and shakers, Robert Frost and Archibald MacLeish appeared in its pages. But except for excerpts in reviews, I have been able to find no appearances of Yeats, Pound, Eliot, Cummings, Stevens, or William Carlos Williams, and when Marianne Moore was reviewed in an early *Phoenix Nest* column, she was dismissed as not a poet but rather an essayist.

Perhaps the near is always the least visible, yet Harriet Monroe in Chicago saw early what *SRL* never recognized, though it was there to be seen. The last few years of our poetry have been a time of consolidation, with minor technical variations, but without the excitement of a true poetic radicalism.

Can we guess whether or not a new poetry is at hand?

28

Certainly some sort of revolution continues in American art and music. If there is to be significant change, there must be an avant-garde, including a lunatic fringe. But where is that avant-garde? If it does exist, it has taken it sixty years to be behind the avant-garde of the twenties.

Good poems are being written. Dozens of rich anthologies have appeared recently, all with excellent poems, even important poems, but none in which we can yet recognize the language and forms of a new sensibility.

Certainly a poet can be a major figure without being a revolutionary; Keats was one. Every major poet will carry poetry where it has not been before, as Keats did, as Roethke did, as some still writing among us are doing perhaps more than we realize, because we have not always recognized greatness among us.

But whatever is happening, it is not revolution. Revolution does not come in any art until those who practice it can no longer express themselves honestly in the ways they were born to. If poets writing in any time can do this, they will. The revolution comes of its own necessity; it cannot be forced.

These times do not seem to be at a cardinal point for the kind of shift in sensibility that leads to great new breakthroughs in poetry; until we reach that point, we must wait upon the kind of greatness that takes poetry into new conceptual dimensions. In time, it will come.

Twentieth-Century Poetry
and Nineteenth-Century Readers

OBERT Frost was like a horse trader. He
would pick up an idea and whittle at it
until he ended up with either a little whittled shape or a
pile of shavings on the floor. One night he got to whittling
around with what he called his "technical tricks." He read
a poem and then asked the audience what meter it was in.
He scolded everybody because they didn't know it was
in hendecasyllabics—which don't work in English anyway.
He discussed all his technical devices, and the more he
talked, the more a lady in the second row bubbled. By the
time he finished, she was at a full boil and immediately
raised her hand. "Mr. Frost," she said, "surely when you
write one of your lovely poems, you are not thinking of
technical tricks!" Frost looked at her a while and said, "I
revel in them!"

There is no other way. Over and over again the poet is
trying to make something, but the audience wants it looser
than that. It is like listening to music by taking a shower

in the sound without thinking of what tradition is being played against, what the structure of the music is, or what the mind of the musician is doing. Poetry is a multiple engagement. It is hard to get at, partly because poetry is so often badly taught by teachers who are forever asking us to say that a poem is beautiful, to paraphrase it into something else, or to make a moral message of it.

As a part of this misconception, the prejudice persists that if a poet is interested in techniques, somehow it's at the peril of the poet's soul. It's as if a musician were in danger of destroying his music by paying attention to the notes.

There is an apocryphal story about Michelangelo and one of his patrons who finally wangled an invitation to dinner. He sat there with Michelangelo and a number of other Roman artists, waiting for a feast of beauty. One man got to talking about what a pirate Brocci was; the price he was charging for his canvas was ridiculous, but it was the only good canvas in Rome, and you had to pay his price. They went on talking about the qualities of various kinds of canvas. Another man had figured out a way to sharpen his chisels to get a particular texture in marble, which brought up the fact that there was a particular piece of Carrara up for auction which was a beautiful piece but had a funny flaw. This sort of conversation went on all evening, and as they left, the patron in some uncertainty said, "You talked about nothing but trifles." I cherish Michelangelo's answer. He said, "Perfection is made of a million trifles." That is the only moral engagement finally that makes one an artist.

Poetry in particular has the merit of being an impure art. It is always impure, and its greatness is in that. We are tugged in all sorts of directions, but this combination of words and devices, diction, metaphor, rhythms, rhymes, and structures is always trying to state a human position. What it demands of the audience is not simply a kind of loose affirmation. It is something much more difficult than that, but joyously difficult. It is much better than easy.

This is the play impulse of poetry, and it extends into all sorts of areas. It is a seminal concept. Poets take on difficulties for the joy of it. This is a basic human impulse. When children draw a hopscotch diagram on the sidewalk, the object is not to step on the lines. Obviously, it would be easier not to step on the lines if you didn't draw them in the first place, but it would be no fun. You impose difficulty because that's where the joy is. Difficulties are invented because without them there is no pleasure.

Every game ever invented by a human being is an arbitrary imposition of difficulty for its own sake.

So the most primitive basis of pleasure in poetry is to abide by the difficulties you have taken on. Frost had a great definition of freedom in aesthetics. This is a part of what he meant when he said that "freedom is moving easy in the harness."

What you must expect from an artist, it seems to me, is a change of imagination. That is difficult and is hard to endure. Most people get their first exposure to poetry in college and are enraptured by Keats. Thereafter Keats remains rich to them, and anything that doesn't sound like Keats is somehow anti-poetry. They have gotten their imaginations in that register, but they can't endure a change into other registers.

Let me take an example from nineteenth-century music. A full orchestral piece by Brahms is likely to come to rest with a whole full-dress parade of final chords. The orchestra keeps going thump, cutathump, cutathump, cutathump, and then it starts over again. Finally it ends in a full blare, all stops out, hammered, central tonic. I don't dislike that kind of music, far from it. But you have to be rather sure of what universe you are living in before you can get that assertive, that conclusive about it. It has to be a fairly closed and positive sense of life you bring to that final tonic chord.

I submit that it is harder and harder these days for thoughtful people to come to such unqualified conclusions. Contemporary music does not sound like a full-dress parade of final chords. It more often sounds like a meander of introductory phrases all the way through, and that is a damnation if you like. Sometimes it is unsatisfying to listen to anything that stays that tentative, but there is a reason for it. At the same time that Bartók was exploring atonality, spending ten years finding out what it was he had been exploring and putting together a theory of it, painters had already broken away from representation, and poets were giving up their tacked-on morals.

Nineteenth-century poetry is full of them. The last four lines or six lines give you the examination answer: "A primrose by a roof's brim, A yellow prim-rose was to him, And it was nothing more"; or "Have I not reason to lament what Man has made of Man?"

Were you an honest, serious, sensitive, intellectual person of Wordsworth's time, it would be possible to believe any number of things that an honest, sensitive, intelligent, intellectual person of our times cannot believe without doubt. Wordsworth never had to worry about Freud. Once you have read Freud there are certain ideas you cannot ignore. You may combat them, you may be bitterly set against them, but you must recognize them as some kind of reality. Once this set of ideas has been loosed, it can no longer be ignored, unless you are insensitive.

And so for Darwin. And so for Karl Marx, who set loose a series of ideas that have to be answered and met. They cannot be ignored. It was possible for a person of Wordsworth's time to be more easily serene than for a thoughtful person of our time. I am not against serenity, but 150-year-old serenity is not a way to live in the world we know.

Art always has to live in a felt world. It has no reality unless it does. If we are not confused, we have not been thinking. The only way to get clarified and put away is to stop the mind. This is the subject of Frost's "Mending Wall." Muriel Rukeyser had a fine phrase for it, "the armored and concluded mind." It is not the mind from which art can come. The mind of the artist has to be venturesome, it has to be open, and it has to respond to the way people live.

One day, for instance, the international revolution in painting called *Cézanne* began, music became a little slower and began to break out into other ways of going, such as the twelve-tone scale, architecture finally felt free from the Greek temple, and science broke itself open into fantastic confusions.

The same thing happened in poetry. When the certainty of the tonic resolution broke down, all sorts of other things had to be found. We have now music that doesn't conclude; it just stops. It is shocking in a sense. It's honest, and it's ours. One of my long-time favorite jazz artists has been Sidney Bechet; what would I do with a fully resolved "Muskrat Ramble"? It would be an insult to the nature of the piece. It has to break off, because any formal resolution attached to this structure would be a lie. It would speak of another way of going, another tempo, another form of things.

We get our resolutions now on dying falls, like the ending of Eliot's "The Hollow Men."

> This is the way the world ends
> Not with a bang but a whimper.

It is a way of stating us.

Supposing a man had been born fifty years ago with the natal sensibilities of a Wordsworth, how would he be different? Supposing Wordsworth had been born in our time, how would he be different? We can read Stephen Spender and find out. Spender is a poet very close to Wordsworth in his sensibilities but with moral identifications real to the life of his own time. He had to engage doubts that were not presented to Wordsworth, to find his attitude toward them. This is a moral problem if you like, but artistically, if one is going to write poetry, it is also an aesthetic problem.

It is too late to write as Tennyson wrote. When Tennyson was not being a very bad poet, he was being a very good one, and when he was being very good, he did that sort of thing better than anyone else. But if he were alive today, he would not write in the same way. He would find a new way of writing to express our new conflicts. What music has been doing, what painting has been doing, what poetry has been doing is shaping forms that will express how we live.

Let us get away from intellectual arguments and put it another way. Imagine a farmer of Wordsworth's time, born on a piece of land that had belonged to his grandfather, and his grandfather, and his grandfather. On that piece of land, he would be doing about the same thing that his fathers as far back as he could know had been doing. He would develop an unquestioned sense that life was a repetition of basic simplicities, and he would transmit this assurance to his own children: this is the farmer's life forever. One simply takes his place in this assured and serene pattern. If you are living in that sort of continuity, it is easy to come by certain serenities. But that continuity has been badly shaken, for the poet as for the farmer.

It is not by accident that E. E. Cummings began to fracture things on the page. It is not by accident that Ezra Pound was writing, "The age demanded an image of its own accelerated grimace." There is a sense of grimace in the age. It is not by accident that Garcia Lorca said, "Hell must be a city very much like New York." We cannot deal with the loss of innocence by writing pastoral poetry or other-wise raising ourselves to lofty places.

The poetry of the nineteenth century was a poetry pri-marily of high seriousness, as Cleanth Brooks called it in his excellent book, *Poetry and the Tradition*. The nineteenth-century poet seemed to be composing hymns. There are many dangers in such a tone, one being that what is even slightly disjunct cannot fit in. Shelley gets going on a poem of high rapture then gets to the line, "thy lips oh slippery blisses," and the poem won't take it. It cannot stand discord.

On the other hand, such a poet as John Donne, whose time, two hundred years earlier, was nevertheless closer to ours in sensibility, could build a poem that is essentially the knocking of two discords into a harmony. He is reaching for all sorts of disparate experiences to bring into a unit. That is the force of the poetry of it. Every time speaks to itself. When I took a course in eighteenth-century poetry at the University of Michigan, professor Louis Bredvold used to say that the eighteenth century was the age of tears. He said that there were more tears shed per capita in that one-hundred years than in any similar period in human history. I am not sure but what the nineteenth century is the cen-tury of long, flowing, black hair. Yet look through all that flowing hair of the romantics, and you will never find a flea. London was not the most sanitary of cities and, sooner or later, the lover must have noticed some fauna on his be-loved. Only Robert Burns bothered to note it, just once in a hundred years. Poets suppressed that view of things.

On the other hand, Donne could write a serious poem called "The Flea," in which he and his beloved are lying in bed together. She reaches out to kill a flea, and he stops her. "Wait!" he says, "This flea is a symbol of our marriage. It has bitten me, it has bitten you, our two bloods are mingled in it." It comes out a serious poem; playfully se-

37

rious, seriously playful, but it is meant; it is not just a joke. No nineteenth-century poet could handle that impulse.

We will have to endure a change of imagination. Poets are looking for forms that will express us in our time. That is why they have tended to rebuff the nineteenth century, in the same way that the American Revolution rebuffed English jurisprudence, still keeping a great deal of it. There is never a complete break with the past. Twentieth-century poets reached across the nineteenth century to the seventeenth, and they found in the metaphysical poets a way of going that would allow them more complexity, that would allow realities to bump heads together.

If anything has been declared as a law of human behavior since Freud, it is ambivalence. People have always been ambivalent, but before Freud it was possible for them to tell themselves that they weren't. They could pretend single motives were single. We know very well now that everything we do comes of mixed motives.

We are constantly in this tug. We have simultaneous and opposite feelings. I submit that symbolism is the natural language for that state of being. I am guessing that the reason the French symbolists have had so powerful an effect upon twentieth-century poets is that symbolism is the natural way for expressing these areas of fear.

Poetry is the shape hidden in an accidental thing, the shape that hides these changes with our relationship to our world. The shapes our poetry takes today have to allow for disjunction. Our poetry has to allow for changing tempo. It has to allow for the vague distaste we have about so much that surrounds us. Serenity is too simple for that.

Fossil Poems *

To the best of my knowledge, it was Richard Cheuenix Trench, scholar, early etymologist, and Anglican Archbishop of Dublin, who coined the term "fossil poem" for a word with a striking root image. Such a word is in essence a poetic image by no known author, but rather a pictorial fancy imprinted by the race itself and left imbedded in the language like a fossil in its stratum of time-gone.

Daisy is such a fossil poem from the folk mind of the English-speaking people. At root, it is "day's eye," the eye of day shining brightly in the meadow. No other language uses this image as the label for the daisy. In Italian, it is called *margharita*, from the Greek word, *margaron*, pearl.

* This essay was the seed from which developed *A Browser's Dictionary*, *A Second Browser's Dictionary*, and *Good Words to You*, all published by Harper & Row, and the National Public Radio program, *Good Words to You*.

And so in French *margharite*, German *margerte*, and Spanish *margarita*, in which form it doubles for a tequila cocktail, the basic image being of a round glass with a clear center and a rim caked with salt into which the wet glass has been dipped. A pearl does very well as a pictogram for a daisy, but I will yet prefer the poetic imagination of "day's eye."

Cowslip is another fossil poem, though more earthy, and of the English folk imagination. The flower is most commonly found in meadows used by cows, and tends to grow close to one of the pancakes that slip out of the cow. Evidence and surveillance: where the cow slips, there slip I.

Every folk imagination uses pictures as the root of some words. The herb we call *rosemary* is not a rose, nor has it anything to do with Mary. The name is based on Latin *ros marina*, sea dew. I don't know what "sea dew" is, but I do find in it a frothy salty suggestion. No one is sure what flower was first identified by this elusive but suggestive root image. Many of our flower names have been used to label different flowers in different ages. *Primrose* is a root from the Latin, *prima rosa; rosa* is a generic name for "flower," hence "first flower" (of spring). No one knows what flower so-labeled was found first. In Old French, this root image seems to have been attached to the hollyhock, certainly not the "first flower," as the primrose is not. Were we accurate in binding our words, it would probably be the crocus or the earliest violet that would bear the name "first flower" (of spring).

Words achieved by combining pictures are everywhere in our modern vocabularies. Following the Civil War, the United States embarked on the transcontinental railroad. The western end was built largely by immigrant labor. The eastern end, built by other immigrants, primarily by the newly numerous Irish, and these eastern laborers were called *gandy dancers.* They lined up along the right-of-way swinging their tools in long rhythmic lines, like tribal dancers. And most of the tools they used were stamped *GANDY* after the now defunct Gandy Manufacturing Company of Chicago. The brand is a natural bit of poetry. It has also made it into American balladry, in a once popular jig tune that ran, in part:

> We danced on the ceiling and we danced on the wall
> At the gandy dancers' ball.

Someone must have made that first poetic observation—and a lovely rich image it is—but today, to all effect, the name is a fragment of a poem sprung from the language itself.

What happens, happens fast. I was on Saipan as an air crew member when the Japanese surrender terms were signed in Tokyo Bay aboard the battleship *Missouri* in mid-September of 1945. By the third or fourth of October, just a touch over two weeks later, I was a civilian on the streets of San Francisco with a discharge button in my lapel.

That discharge button represented the American eagle alighting, as seen now on a dollar bill and a U. S. officer's visored cap: stylized rampant, its head in profile between spread wings, its legs spread to either side, and talons clutching arrows on its left, an olive branch on its right.

For the discharge button, a disaster of official art, the eagle shed its arrow. It was shown in full-body profile as having just landed, one leg forward and the other back, its wings not yet entirely closed. The result was a grotesquely clumsy waddling eagle with its wings ajar. As if inevitably, it came to be known as the "ruptured duck." There is something stunningly poetic in the speed with which the name attached itself to the ludicrous official bauble. I had mine within three weeks of the official final surrender, and the name "ruptured duck" was already firmly established in American-English use.

Indo-European was an ancestral language brilliantly deduced from the roots common to its descendant tongues. We do not know much about the syntax of Indo-European, but two centuries of meticulous scholarship have persuasively fixed the root elements of its words. Indo-European was in use about 6000 B.C. In it, the root *ni* meant "down." It still so functions with a slight vowel shift and a common suffix in English *nether*, meaning low or below. The root *sed*, still visible in *sedan* and *sedentary*, meant "to sit." A later root, probably a millenium or two later, combined these elements into the root *nezde*, literally, "at down," but specifically associated with birds, whence the Latin *nidies*, "nest," which is to say "place where the bird sits down."

The form survives in Italian *nido*, French *nide*, nest, and also in the language of British gamekeepers for a "batch" of game birds, as in *a nide of pheasants*, signifying at root as many as hatch from one nest, though the term is now also used for "the season's hatch," the total of new birds in a given game preserve.

The same ancient root, *nizde*, went into common Germanic, which is to say pre-written German. The first Germanic runes are from about the third century B.C. *Nizde*, therefore, had three or four thousand years in which to evolve by oral transmission before the form is attested in Old English and German writing as "nest."

Our Germanic language fathers, however, noted that where the bird sits, it drips. In the rites of spring, the nest is liberally besmeared. In hot summer it reeks. To express this condition, Common Germanic added an adjectival suffix that may be inferred from Dutch *nestich* and Old English *nestig*, "nest-like," which is to say "bestial and stinking," and so, with minor modifications, our word *nasty*, which you may now use as precisely as you please.

A well-known but often confused etymology traces *trivia* to Latin *tri viae*, the intersection of three streets; streets (within the city), not cross-country highways. Where three streets intersect they form a small *plaza* (in Italian, *piazza*), or a *largo*, a wide place (cf. *large*), and *piazza* and *largo* are natural places for a street market. Did one buy only cheap *shoddy* at street markets? So some explain, but most of what was up for sale was food, most of it good and much of it delicious, as fruit in full tree-ripened season.

The English sense of *trivia*, I suggest, was from the local gossip exchange of the housewives who made a social ritual of their morning and afternoon visits to the market. Meeting as they did twice daily, they were seldom equipped with weighty new topics of discussion, but the lack of anything to say has never held down the word count of the devoted gossip.

One will have to dig a bit deeper to trace the origin of *liquid*. It derives from Latin *liquere*, "to be liquid," "to liquefy." The Latin form is based on the combined Indo-European stem *lein-wo*, "to go away." A liquid is that form of matter that goes away. The root does not explain how a liquid departs. It may flow away, it may evaporate, or it may percolate into the soil. There is an ambiguity in the roots of this fossil poem, but it works as sweetly as the consonant ambiguities of a poem.

The root sense will also explain the various English words that follow from *delinquere*, which is *linquere* with the nasal infix. To be delinquent is, at root, "to go away" from the accepted standards of behavior.

And then, because there was a felt need for distinct labels, a variant gave us *liquor*, an opulent liquid, and *liqueur*, the French form of the same word, for after-dinner drinks generally more flavorful than spirituous. Language invents what it needs when it needs it.

It is an impoverishment to think of words as static labels.

Language is a process of constant change. I came upon my image of process some years ago when I sat in on a film about the zinnia. The botanist-photographer had fixed his camera on the spot shooting single frames at intervals of some hours. When these frames were projected at normal forward speeds, it made a film that I guess to have lasted for a bit over twenty minutes.

What I saw was not zinnia-as-object but zinnia-as-process. And never still. A shoot poked through what I guess was potting soil, it reached and side-budded, then swelled at the top and unfolded a bloom that held itself wide to the sun, then slowly sagged away and down to become dead stalks at the end of its twenty-minute-and-a-bud season.

I have grown zinnias. I had never really seen one before this film. I wonder what a copper beech would be, so parsed and then animated. I am ready to believe that we know nothing until we have seen it a process-in-process.

That zinnia-in-process is a natural image for language-in-process. At the end of the sixteenth century, the Dutch were pre-eminent in European politics, naval and military power, commerce, philosophy, and the arts. Literally hundreds of words and phrases passed from Dutch into English, among them *bully*, only slightly modified from Dutch *boele* (in Dutch *oe* is pronounced like the *oo* of English *loop*). The original sense of *bully* taken directly from Dutch was "sweetheart" and also "fine figure of a man." A bully was originally every girl's Mister Right.

In early seventeenth-century English, the sense of bully developed from "fine figure of a man," to "coxcomb, pretentious young fop," and in the late seventeenth century, the word had acquired such senses as "swindler," "card shark," "hypocrite"—a man so obviously overdressed as to imply deceit.

In the eighteenth century, the word added the sense

"pimp," which is akin, of course, to the original "sweetheart" but now with a criminal association, one who trades commercially in sweethearts of a sort. In the nineteenth century, *bully* meant primarily "strong-arm man, thug" (one of Boss Tweed's bully boys). Today, *bully* labels one who intimidates weaker people, either by physical violence or psychic coercion.

But what about Theodore Roosevelt's constant use of *bully!* as an exclamation of enthusiastic approval? In that exclamatory usage, the word was back to its sixteenth-century Dutch senses, "sweetheart" and "fine figure of a man," an enthusiastic reassertion of Roosevelt's Dutch ethnic roots.

Sometimes the trace is certain and yet obscure. The root of our word *book* is certainly from Indo-European *bhag, bhago,* "beech tree." A book is a volume of bound pages, usually with printing or writing on them. But "bound pages" is a late sense, and such a thing was probably not seen in the Northland until the first missionaries arrived from Rome, sometime around the late sixth century A.D. The first known "writing" among the Germanic peoples was not writing but rune carving. Most surviving runes have been cut into metal or chiseled on stone. But the earliest carvings, of which a few examples survive, were on staves of wood. Beech is an even-grained, easily washed hardwood. Robert Frost knew the virtues of hardwoods, and cited them in "Two Tramps in Mud Time":

> Good blocks of oak it was I split
> As large around about as the chopping block,
> And every piece I squarely hit
> Fell splinterless as a cloven rock.

The etymological connection of block and book was by a simple third century A.D. interpretation "what one writes

on." There is certainly no evidence that blocks of beech—
or blocks of oak, for that matter—were shaved thin and
written on with ink. Writing with ink came later, with
those first missionaries from Rome. Runes were carved.

Sometimes the root suggestion is like a glimpse into early
history. *Lord*, as a title of dominance, of nobility, as the
landholder (this sense still surviving in landlord), was in
Old English *hlāfweard*. Old English *hlāf* survives in slightly
altered form as our "loaf," but earlier it referred to most all
bread. *Weard* survives in warder and warden. The old *hlāfweard* was the guardian of the food on an estate, the one
under whose guardianship one drew his bread. An early
rune, probably fourth century A.D., renders the sense *bread
giver*: "but I, Viv, engraved these runes to my bread-giver
(i.e., lugelord), Voldrid."

And so "lady" from Old English *hlāfdaege*, literally, "one
who kneads bread," which is to say, "she who has the keys
to the larder," which is to say, "mistress of the house."

And what are we to make of the fact that *true* is ultimately from Indo-European *dreu*, tree. Is it enough to
render that verbal idea as "self-evident as a tree?" I doubt
that it is, at least until one has fixed on the religious fact
that the early Teutons were tree-worshipping *druids*. *Druid*
derives from *dreu*, as above, combined with *wit*, to see, to
understand. A *druid* was "one who understood about trees,"
which is to say, one who could propitiate and summon the
daemons of trees and of the forest. The "truth" of nature
and of existence was in the tree spirits, and what the tree-
wise Druid priest summoned from the trees was the truth.
Now, perhaps, one may say that *true* is, at root, "self-
evident as a tree," but only when one remembers that the
gods are in this.

The process of change is the process of being. *Imp* originally meant a plant shoot, a graft. It is based on Greek *im-*

phein, "to graft a vegetable shoot." In falconry one still "imps" feathers into a flight-damaged wing to improve its flying characteristics. In fourteenth- and fifteenth-century English, one might refer formally to "his gracious majesty and the royal imp" (the prince). The spelling would have been a touch different, but the phrasing given has the gist of it.

Gist is based on the Old French tombstone inscription *ci giste,* "here lies," the rendering of Latin *hic jacet.* By the time *ci giste* goes on the stone and the stone on the grave, one has about had the gist of it. *Jectare* is also ultimately the root of *ghetto,* the section of the city in which Jews were once forced to live.

I know of no English dictionary that has traced *ghetto* to its source; the Latin *jactere* means "to throw" and also "to cast, as in a foundry."

The first European ghetto was decreed in Venice in the early sixteenth century, and its site was the island on which stood the Venetian foundry, or *geto.* A few English etymologists have referred to Venetian *geto* but shied away from it on the assumption, first, that it would be pronounced in English as if it were "jet-o," and second, that the hard "g" in Italian tends to soften to a "j" sound, but the "j" does not harden to the "g" sound as in go. What these sources have overlooked is that in the peculiarities of Venetian dialect, *geto* was in fact pronounced with a hard "g." There is even a bastardized sixteenth-century church-Latin form, *ghectum.*

And to confuse things further, Jewish scholars have cited Hebrew *get,* "divorce," and have etymologized *geto* as meaning "place of our divorcement." This rendering is certainly ingenious. What it overlooks is that *geto,* or *ghetto,* is the result of a Latin-Italian evolution and not answerable to the senses of Hebrew. This is etymology as my aged Uncle Alessio once had it in his favorite political oration, a set

47

piece that was touched off whenever he was reminded of pay toilets and of the fact that a soul in need had to pay five cents to answer a call of nature. "She's a free goundree (free country)," Uncle would orate, "she's a freeza you, an' a freeza me, an' a freeza evrebodee thatsa the free goundree."

But to have done with *ghetto*, the "h" was inserted about the mid-sixteenth century to conform to standard Italian (not Venetian) orthography, and at about the same time, the "t" was doubled under the influence of *-etto*, the common diminutive suffix. As I say, no dictionary in English has tracked down this etymology, but that is how the word came about.

Always process. How can one miss the sense of process on reading in William Langland's *Piers Plowman* (late fourteenth century), "and buxom to the law." He meant "obedient," "yielding," and even "servile to the law." The form is based on Old English *bugan*, to bow, to bow down to, to yield. With intermediate early Middle English forms *ybuccsome, bogsum*, and finally *buxom(e)*, the word came to mean all the traits an Old English lordling most desired in his servants—servile obedience and the bodily strength to drudge on cheerfully and tirelessly. Through the sixteenth century, the word could be applied to either sex. Only in the seventeenth, for reasons that still partly elude me, did the word become specific to a hefty big-busted farm wench, and so to bust measurement.

Demijohn, a large bottle usually woven around with reeds, had a similar evolution in French. These bottles towered above the regular bottles at the country inn. Accordingly they came to be called "Dame Jeanne," Dame Jean, a tribute to some impossibly large, slab-sided, and buxom mistress of a country inn. And if the whimsy seems a slight one, it is worth noting that language seizes on what it needs: today easily recognizable cognates of imposing *Dame Jeanne* are standard in Spanish, Italian, Arabic, and English.

48

Or how about Hamlet's "to make the royal bed of Den-mark a couch for cursed luxury." Today *luxury* means "sump-tuous living." To Shakespeare it meant always and only lust. And so Dante's reference to *Cleopatra lussuriosa*. The root sense is "lush, rampant, unrestrained vegetable growth." Dante meant exactly that Cleopatra's appetites were un-restrained, unchecked. And so to sexual abandonment, as it is still known to happen in what are called "luxury apartments."

So *artificial*, as late as the seventeenth century, meant "ar-tistic." So *starve* long meant "any slow lingering death." So Chaucer's "Christe sterfed on the crosse," Christ "starved," i.e., underwent a painful lingering death on the cross. Then the process took over. Towns were subjected to a slow, lingering death in siege warfare; they were "starved out" in the root sense. Such towns, however, had water and shelter. What tended to give out first was food. And so "death by food deprivation," one of the many early senses took over the whole word.

Focus began as the Latin word for hearth. Don't trust your Latin dictionary if it defines it as fireplace. The Ro-mans had no fireplaces as we know them. They had firepits in which they burned charcoal, and perhaps some early form of coal—the record is obscure on that point of con-vergence, and so our English sense of "focal point," but the word passed into Italian as *fuoco*, fire, and into Old French as *feu*. And so *curfew*, at root *courve feu*, a common medi-eval night signal to cover the household fires, a custom that became law after several medieval towns were gutted by night fires.

Fornication is from Latin *fornus*, an oven. *Fornicate* is also an architectural adjective describing a kind of arch or vault resembling the brickwork in the cellars of some Roman public buildings. The poor and the prostitutes took up hovels among these cellar works. So *fornicatus* originally meant this arched brickwork, but in church Latin, *forni-catio* came to mean the act of visiting a whore among the cellar brickwork. Ovens were once commonly made of such brickwork. In Italian *forno* means oven.

The *sad* of *sadirons* (heavy irons) is a curious survival. The sense "heavy" occurs again in "Fate struck him a sad blow." I once heard a Virginia matron apologize because "the bread had *sad streaks* in it." She meant that it had not been properly kneaded, and that some parts of the dough had not risen. In British, *sad cake* is cake soaked with (made heavy by) rum or brandy. These are all colloquial rather than standard forms.

The root is Indo-European *sa*, "to be replete." So Latin *satur*, "satiety." And so English sated. Old English *saed* meant weary. Modern English *sad* means low in spirits. The root *sa* has never had the primary sense "heavy." Yet to be sated is to be heavy with food; to be *saed*, weary, is to be heavy with fatigue; to be sad is to be heavy of heart. Folk English has understood that implicit (never primary) sense and has preserved it in the colloquial forms cited above.

Dilapidated is at root the Latin *dis*, apart, away from, with *lapidare*, to throw stones. *Dilapidatus* means to have stones fallen from. The coliseum is dilapidated in a strict sense. One could argue etymologically that people who were stoned were dilapidated. The new morality of revolutionary Iran's leaders was somewhat signaled when three sluts and three dirty old men were sentenced to be buried with only their heads above ground and then stoned to death. They died dilapidated. But one who knows the word to its root would avoid a reference to dilapidated old clothes—unless perhaps the reference is to the caryatids.

One of my sons, once, referring to one of his friends, said, "that dude is out of his furrow." It was my general impression that all of his friends were out of their furrows, but what caught my attention was the fact that his slang had exactly duplicated the Latin roots *de,* "out of" and *lira,* "furrow." The Latin *delinoare* came to mean "to rant and rave," but the root image is "out of the furrow," i.e., "plowing not in a straight line but loopingly all over the field." And so our word *delirious.*

And then, too, the lovely root of *inchoate* from Latin *in cohum* meaning at root "hitched up but not yet plowing." A plow was *in cohum* when the plow harness was attached to the yoke of a team of oxen.

The moral-minded will want to argue that it is useful to know words as this sort of process. I have no doubt that to register English words and phrases in process is to use them more accurately, but I am not inclined to argue utility as if it justified the pleasure in language for its own sake. I suppose one could argue that one who has read Shakespeare closely can be expected to write good business letters, but if that is a good reason for reading Shakespeare, it is the least of good reasons, and in fact a piddling one. The one truly good reason is for pleasure.

And so for language in process. Everything is a distant second to the joy of responding to words as living process. Nothing of mankind is more characteristic than the language process. Nor am I persuaded that mankind amounts to much. Certainly a more admirable species might have descended to something a touch more admirable than we are. Yet we are all we have, and there is nothing in which we have moments more splendid than these in which we turn out to be the language-makers.

The roots of that process are hidden just under our daily notice. Have you a *credenza* in your house? Why should a sideboard be called, at root, a credence? Because in the days when poisoning was a common political ploy—what the Italians learned tolerantly to call not murder but *una morte assistata,* an assisted death—food was set on a sideboard and not served at table until a trusted servant had given it credence by tasting some of each dish and bottle.

Salver, a commonly silver tray on which the butler once delivered mail to the master, is from Latin *salvare,* which came to mean "to taste," but which at root is "to make safe" and by extension "to insure one's health," as in the common Latin greeting *salve,* in effect, "health to you." The salver was originally the tray on which the taster placed the food he was to taste before it was served.

Butler also derives from this cautionary service. *Butler* derives etymologically from the same source as bottle. But the ancient butler was not only the chief steward of a royal family, but the lord's taster and cupbearer, and a trusted member of the royal "cabinet."

So in Genesis 40:21, "he restored the chief butler unto his butlership again: and he gave the cup into Pharoah's hand."

Call that useful knowledge if you wish. But before all else I mean to cherish it as a memorable sequence from the language-in-process movie. With a little tuning of the attention, that movie can play forever in the theater of the mind's eye.

Or, to get back to the beginning, every paragraph can be read as an anthology of poetry, and so all our reading— even of poetry itself—will be richer for it.

For the Love of Language

INTELLIGENCE, I submit, begins with the
ability to see essential likenesses and essential
differences. But that is only the first class in intelligence,
freshman intelligence. From there on, the second kind has
to operate, and that is the ability to see likenesses and differences within likenesses, because two things may be similar in many ways but different in others; if elementary intelligence begins with grasping rough overriding similarities,
certainly the rest of the process of education addresses the
ability to see differences within the likenesses and likenesses within differences. There is no end to this; it is a
constant experiment. But this is all right; I want to think of
education as a storehouse. What a culture stores up and
what is transmitted within that culture is a memory that the
race has developed.

The difference between a civilized person and a savage
simply is the fact that the savage has not received enough
news from mankind. The problem is to get that person

53

in touch with continuity, sometimes called the Great Tradition.

Suppose that every generation of chemists had to start over again from scratch and make every chemical discovery again. We never would get anywhere. As it stands now, by the time a boy finishes a high school course in chemistry, he knows more than leading chemists in the past knew all their lives. The first course in chemistry is a course in history; we go through a series of chemical problems in chronological order with the idea that we will sometime catch up with the chemical history of the past, and if we stay with it long enough, we'll be able to make history of our own. At the beginning, every science course is a course in history.

I am persuaded that in our high schools and colleges the elementary sciences, that is, the first steps of the sciences, are much better taught than are the humanities, as a general rule. Or to simplify it, let's say that high school chemistry, by and large, is taught much better and in a more efficient way than is high school English. I think the reason for that is in the subject. It is not necessary for a high school teacher of chemistry to be a human being. It is not forbidden; it is simply not necessary. Any mechanical demonstrating device could have taken me through the thirty-two experiments I performed in my high school chemistry course.

In teaching poetry, it is necessary to see some of the things poetry can do. To begin with, the native dimension of poetry is language. A poet not only uses language, he uses more of the language than anybody else. In conversation we tend to use the surface of the language, but language is a very awesome thing. In our conversation, words lose their distinction as they get used too cheaply. "Like" and "as" have become practically synonymous. I expect that in the year 2000, Shakespeare will have written a play called "Like You Like it."

I don't think there is any activity more profoundly human than the use of language. What would any of us be without language? Words, to be sure, are not the only language we have. Music is a language; dance is a language; painting is a language. I have seen a mechanic carrying on a perfect conversation with an engine. Imagine what civilization would be, what we would be, what our national institutions would be, what our lives would be, if we did not have our languages! Words most of all go deeply into us; a person haunted by language or words is somehow brought into the presence of the way we think. The words themselves, the rhythm of words that fall together, the enormous rhythm of poetry, is an awakening force. I will insist that once we get language into our heads, once we know what a human being sounds like, we are ready to be human.

Survival

I USED to write important poems. In the last years of the 1930s at the University of Michigan everyone wrote important poems. The young know no limits when they are given a blueprint of the future, a hatful of slogans, and the assurance that they are about to save the world. In 1938 or 1939, Alfred Kreymborg appeared on a panel in New York City to discuss the future of the American Theater and found it possible to say that the discussion was all nonsense because in three or four years the Communist Revolution would have taken place and reshaped America to the inevitability of dialectical materialism. No one laughed him off the stage. Intellectuals were used to hearing such important declarations, and many were conditioned to believe them.

And there was the Spanish War. Spain was the Vietnam of my college years. It gave rise to tens of thousands of important bad poems. Some linked the agony of the Loyalists with the Communist Revolution, and certainly there was a connection. I found I could have deep feelings about the fight, probably inspired by the few wounded veterans of the Lincoln Brigade who had become students at Michigan. I could have those feelings while pondering deep doubts about the important statements made by the communists. But one way or another, we all had important convictions to utter.

(I signed every petition and ironically those signatures saved my life. They were collected and filed away by the House Committee on Un-American Activities, generally known, after its chairman, as the Dies Committee. In 1942, I completed my cadet training as an aerial navigator and was given an honorable discharge to accept a commission. The day before commissioning I was busted to private on orders of the Dies Committee as a P.A.F., a premature antifascist. P.A.F., hard as it may be to believe it, was an official designation. It was based on the assumption that anyone opposed to Hitler before our declaration of war was probably a communist fellow traveler or communist sympathizer. My flight was sent to the Eighth Air Force in England. A year later, every man I had trained with was either killed in action or missing. I could not resist sending Martin Dies a thank you letter.)

Back at pre-war University of Michigan, there was more. There were the bloody battles between the auto workers and Ford's private security force headed by Harry Bennett, Bennett's goons scoring a hideous victory at the Battle of the Overpass, and *Time* featuring bloody photo spreads of union leaders, among them Walter Reuther.

All these things and more left intellectuals feeling that there were important things to say. They felt important to me, and the fact that I hardly knew what I was talking about made no difference. My sense of decency was ablaze.

Let me indulge myself in the comforting dramatic pose that I am a survivor. I have survived religion, the combined efforts of the American and the Japanese Air Forces to get me shot down, political activism, and even, I think, ambition. I have no worlds to keep and none to save. What I have left is a few more years and in them some lovingly absorbing work of no consequence except to me. I am learning to write unimportant poems. If I can make them small enough, I may get them down to life size. That isn't much. I am more or less stuck with being a member of the human race, which itself isn't much, except that it is all there is, and therefore everything. It isn't much, but any race that can produce an Archibald MacLeish has at least set a standard for itself. And like it or not, we have nothing else to invest in.

I write unimportant poems because I am human and gross and have nothing to say. I am, however, a language supplicant. The language is wiser, deeper, more sentient, and more haunted than anyone who uses it. I mean only to woo the language, to submit myself to it as best I can, and to hope that when I have hearkened to it humbly and gratefully, it will now and then empower me to do what I could never have done when I was important and came to the poem with a half-prepared speech, intending only to raid the language for flourishes.

The ideal poem is a stirring awake of words in a haunted silence. It is not an assertion but a being, a hearkening to being, and a way of being.

It will not do, however, to assume a soulfulness. Poetry and language become haunted only in the passions of the learned. Not in the learning of the musicologist—which I do not scorn—but in the learning of the violinist who has played his life and love into the instrument for its own sake. When it works, it sounds almost as if all the graves of time had opened and that the dead of this race had improvised their truest awareness of life as they remember it.

But let me walk wary of the word "improvise." I have had

students who decided that the one thing above all else was improvisation. I could even agree with them, with the difference that they believed the impromptu was what happened when you sat down to let it spill, whereas I find over the years that the impromptu is what begins to happen slowly at the tenth, fifteenth, or twentieth draft. As Yeats put it in "Adam's Curse":

> . . . a line will take us hours maybe,
> Yet if it does not seem a moment's thought
> Our stitching and unstitching has been naught.

In many young poets I seem to find the assumption that the one prerequisite for poetry is the excitation of ignorance. Excited ignorance is legal, and I mean to be ruled by laws and the Constitution. But time's winged chariot hurries, and I have no time to waste sympathy on what bores me. Decades ago I resigned a professorship because I was weary of being hired sympathy. Having foregone tenure and pension, I will insist I have earned a right to an unassertive selfishness. I will vote for egalitarianism, but I will not be bored by it; I am busy wooing my own ghosts as language allows me to woo them. Donne said it for me: "For God's sake hold your tongue and let me love!" The years left to me are mine, and I do not intend to waste them in debate.

I have, to be sure, had things I wanted to say about society and its quirks and failures. I count it a blessing that for twenty years I wrote a column for the *Saturday Review* and was free to sound off on any cause and cantaker. But I have learned not to send a poem on a prose errand.

It is my poetic faith that if I can stir my own most private ghosts to their root of being, I may hope to reach into an area of the unconscious in which my privacy becomes accordant to every human being's privacy. That seems an ambitious declaration, but it is truly neither an ambition nor a declaration. I mean only that I want to woo my failure in the most absorbing way. I write as an alcoholic drinks, compulsively and for its own sake. I do not care to be sober when I can yet hope to hear the language speak to compulsion.

Still, I never expected anything. I assumed I could always do enough work to earn food and some sort of shelter. And I insisted on writing poems. The one survival I know is to go on writing.

Years ago I wrote a poem about this. I called it "A Black Bread Store." I was in the business of selling coarse and garlicky crusts for which there is not much market. I welcomed customers, to be sure, but when none came, I planned to survive by eating my losses. The plan has not changed.

I have never been tempted by the marketplace because there was no marketplace to tempt me. Remember, we are in the black bread store. Customers are few, if any, and they are not even the reason for starting the bakery. I welcome any recognition so long as I am not required to take it seriously. What I do is done for the doing. I am rich so long as I am able to do what pleases me most, if only to fly paper airplanes into the apocalyptic wastebasket. And let the wastebasket remain the central monument of my life. As Roethke put it, "What slips away provides."

It is relatively easy for a poet to remain pure and true to the poet's calling. Let me testify that I have never been offered a bribe to write badly. I have written badly enough without tenders of subversion. I think it might be thrilling to have some shady muse sidle up to me and say, "Here's $10,000—throw the next poem." I would probably throw the next poem out of natural ineptitude, anyway. The craft is not easy. It is better than easy. It is joyously difficult. Once I had decided the poem was a botch and belonged in the wastebasket, what would there be to keep me from sorting through the pieces and trying once more to reassemble them? The best reason for putting anything on paper, as several different authors have said, is that you may then change it. Changing it into shape is the art and also the passion, and in my experience it is not subject to subornation.

There have been occasional sops. *Playboy* once asked me to write an article on poetry. I have written more than enough maunders on poetry, and though I am no admirer of Hugh Hefner, he was ready to pay about ten times more than I was used to. In every way it seemed to beat digging manholes.

It then turned out that *Playboy* wanted not an article on poetry, but one on how poets make a living, and I lost interest. Digging manholes is one thing; digging graves, another. I don't care how poets make a living. The one reason I know for writing a poem is the probably foregone ideal of writing it as well as possible.

And I do not care—nor should you care—what the poet had to endure to achieve the poem. We care only that it quicken us.

I think there is more. I think that in the nature of our species we are not really sad that Keats died young. We like to pretend to a sadness. I think we are glad he suffered and died—his death saves us the trouble of dying personally, and it allows us a fine resonant emotion about doomed youth. He might, moreover, have lived to be as dull and fumblesome as the aged Tennyson.

These literary sadnesses smack of false convention. When I was flying bomber missions as an aerial gunner, a similar false convention required every survivor to pretend to great sorrow when a friend was shot down. The fact is that I was secretly glad, and so I believe was everyone else. We were staying alive or dying by a blind lottery. It was a matter of how the numbers came up. Mathematics insisted that there be some unknown number of deaths, and every time someone used up one of the deadly numbers, our chances somehow seemed to improve by the removal of one more black ball from the lottery basket. We were alive because men had died, and every new death not ours made us more alive. These responses are not subject to reason. Like a poem, they are from the roots of being. I can say only that I am a species and its ways are mine. I am drawn to poems, in part, because they most teach me what this species is and does. Language, I believe, is the deepest unconscious fantasy of this species.

If death can emerge as a secret pleasure in poetry—as it did for Keats himself when he wrote "When I Have Fears that I May Cease to Be"—what measure can there be in the marketplace? Poetry has nothing to sell and only its illusory notion of perfection to seek. As Wallace Stevens wrote in his eighties (and I quote from memory, perhaps bungling the words, but not the effect), "What has there been to love that I have not loved?" Love is above all the act of wooing the language to a haunted perception, which becomes a way of being, the only survival, for its own glad sake.

Selection, Simultaneity, and Requiredness

THE ESSENTIALS OF POETRY

IT seems to me that at least one of the essential qualities contained in the meaning of a poem is the poet's principle of selection. I don't care what one is writing about; I don't care much what attitude one is taking toward this poem. In a devoted act of writing, there has to be a refusal to make cheap choices. The integrity of that refusal is the final meaning and the final morality of the poem.

When I had been working on Dante for quite some time, I found myself wondering what made his lines poetry. As I read it, it seems to be a rather chunky, eleven-syllable line, sometimes stiff and awkward. Maybe, indeed, it is prose. If it is prose, it is prose so rigorously selected—there is so much mind at work in every turning of the poem—that this is prose of an order to which we are not accustomed. This is what I mean by the principle of selection. When a poet has said four words, he must pick out the fifth. It doesn't just happen. He has to choose it. Everything that gets into a work of art gets in by an act of choice. Every last comma, every variant spelling, every word choice is something that has to be in fact a choice. It does not come in by accident. There may be luck, but the luck of the artist has to be earned.

Let me give one example of what I mean by this. I like to present a class with a poem and leave a blank or two in it. There has to be a choice. Emily Dickinson says of a snake, "When stooping to secure it, It ———— and was gone." Now what's a two-syllable word that would fill in this line? How does a snake move? What is the best word one could find for it? She said "It wrinkled and was gone." My point is that if the student is forced to try his choices against a good one, he begins to realize how much is involved in coming up with a really good choice.

Another good example is a line from Keats' "Epistle to Charles Cowden Clarke," in which Keats is thanking Clarke for having introduced him to the pleasures of poetry. He thanks him for this aspect of poetry, for that aspect of poetry, for other aspects. Along the way he says, "For Spencerian vowels that. . . ." How would you complete that line? What do Spencerian vowels do? Spencerian vowels "that divinely lilt"—that would get you second prize in the women's club competition for spring sonnets. It's too easy a choice. Anybody can say divinely lilt. Spencerian vowels that "enchant the ear"—that is fancy enough, isn't it? But when the real choice comes in, you know it. What Keats wrote was "Spencerian vowels that elope with ease." He got those two Spencerian vowels in there, actually three— "elope with ease"—with the long "ease" and that little slide on the "elope." If a teacher can make students understand that difference between a master choice and a cheap choice, I think a great deal will have been accomplished.

Every order of good choice is a morality. The refusal to do the easy thing, the cheap thing, or the inadequate thing is as much morality as there is. Human beings, we recognize, are verbal animals. If the level at which we select language could be schooled (and poetry is one of the best ways of schooling it), there is no need to teach morality overtly. Let it sneak in. It sticks faster when it sneaks in than when it is plastered on. This, I think, is one of the humanizing functions of the arts. It always hurts me to see poetry gone at as a kind of hammer-and-tongs morality. Morality is not in the subject; it is in the way the poet carries his obligations, his duties, his self-inflicted restrictions. Often he doesn't quite know where they are going.

Another essential quality of poetry is simultaneity. In any work of art, more than one thing is happening at once. I suppose that counterpoint in music is the simplest example. One of the reasons that criticism is always crabbed is that it has to talk about a poem that is doing eight things at once, and talk about those eight things separately, one at a time.

I did an analysis of Frost's "Stopping by Woods on a Snowy Evening" in the *Saturday Review* and I got two groups of outraged letters, among others. One group said in essence "get your big muddy feet off that miracle"—that is, "analysis destroys beauty." I reject that argument as ridiculous on the face of it. The other was "Huh, at last we have caught you out. You are talking about a poem that is only sixteen lines long and you take ten columns to do it." The premise here is, of course, that criticism should not be longer than the thing criticized. And that argument, too, must be dismissed as ridiculous. Criticism has to be longer and more laborious than the thing criticized. If you watch a gull fly for thirty seconds, you then have enough material, if you have watched closely, to write a textbook on aerodynamics. In such a book you would have to have chapters on what the tailfeathers are doing, chapters on what the right wing is doing, on what the left wing is doing, and on their relation to one another. You have to have chapters on how the gull is balancing his body and how it steers with its head. All these things have to be discussed separately and in crabbed detail, but if you get through this crabbed exercise, there is some hope that the next time you look at a gull you may see more. This is the object of criticism, not as an end in itself, but to lead one back to the form so that we can see more of what is going on at the time. Certainly I know of no poem that is a one-minded assertion. More than one thing is forever happening at the same instant within any good poem.

The third central characteristic of poetry is requiredness. Simply stated, one thing in a poem requires another. One thing in a poem calls another into being. If you will think in terms of music, again, you will have no difficulty with this notion. You cannot write the end of a piece of music and then write the beginning. You have to write it in the order in which it comes. You cannot write it backwards. A poem is a self-entering, self-generating, self-sealing form. The poem has ended when you have used up all of your material, just as the use of a tonic chord does in a formal piece of music. By the time you get that last resolution, by the time you have resolved on that final chord, every implication of the music has been put at rest. There are no questions left. The work is a whole, organic thing.

Dear N:

THANKS for your letter and poem. I am glad to hear you are all well and that the baby, having had a look at the human race, can't stop howling. Once any of us has had a look, it's only reasonable to want to go back.

"Back out of all this now too much for us." That's Frost's line. One of the great opening lines of twentieth-century poetry, I think.

And so to your poem.

I've read it. I have some feelings about it. I don't know what to say. It's not that I lack a firm impression of the poem, but how can I, as a would-be critic, say it in any way that you, as a would-be poet, will be willing to receive.

Suppose I told you the poem is great, that you're a genius, and that all the literate world has been waiting for you. Would you believe me? If you have had the least thought of answering "yes," you're a hopeless case. Yet

69

every writer writes to be told something of the sort. There is this ego fuel of us all: when a poet says, "Tell me what you think about this poem I have written," he means, "OK, praise me! Praise me!"

Ego is a basic animal attachment and no more to be apologized for than one's legs. It takes a humping lump of ego for any man to assume he can write a poem toward something like mortal consequence, and your poem, God knows, strains not only at the mortal weight of mankind but into outer space and the universal riddle.

The arrogance of taking oneself seriously enough to write such a poem can be sublimated only by finding in the act of the writing something more important than one's own ego. The medium—form and language—is that more important thing. Even great poets, once away from the medium, can become cantankerous and egotistical asses. But when a poet is absorbed by the medium, it is as if he is wanting for it to speak. He *listens* the poem into being, *from* form and language *into* form and language. He is in some felt sense less the originator of the process than the attendant upon it.

You don't know what I'm talking about, do you? You have had a baby, a miracle to your house—and you have been moved to speak your miracle of feeling. And why bore your miraculous self with thought of your medium? Or is it the medium itself that bores you?

Let's return to ego. You want to be praised:

I really haven't tried much of any poetry before, but I've worked hard at this poem and it feels *right!*

Yes, the italics and the exclamation point are yours. And so is your lie about working hard. The baby was born six days ago. You haven't had a full week yet in which to work out this near fatal solution of the universe, and you call that hard work. Son of man, what you are talking about is not

70

DEAR N:

hard work but only ego excitement. You are stunned by the fact of getting some words on paper, and what you really ask from me is the sort of ovation you have been giving yourself.

You say you really want to know what I think. I think you have written an obviously bad poem, and how can I explain its badness to you? If I say that, having chosen to write metrically, you are hobbled by your metrics—will that be a communication?

If I say that, having chosen to rhyme, you rhyme not your lines but only their last words, straining those last words into place for rhyme purposes rather than letting them fall into inevitable idiomatic place within the line— will that be a communication?

If I tell you that your words do not knit their overtones into one another, or that your metaphoric structure has no plot, or that when you try a metaphor you are so distrustful of it that you immediately restate the purpose of the meta- phor in "overt prose," so to speak—will any of that be a communication?

If your ego is working at something like racial norms, you will probably be thinking I am speaking crabbed nonsense, that you have sent me eternal feeling and I have given you back pedantry.

If you feel any such thing, you are resisting the stuff of poetry. Your feelings remain human enough. I agree that a man's joy at the birth of his first child is more important than the technical management of a poem. Certainly more important to him. Perhaps more important to all of us—for a while. For the while his life and the child's lasts. But if the poem—as, for example, Virgil's fourth *Eclogue*, which also celebrated the birth of a child—is to endure, the child, the father, the occasion disappeared from everything but the poem. They have only the importance the good poem

71

gives them. And good poems are written not simply by human beings, but by a special sort of human being with a
special sensitivity to his medium, a joyous sense of lifetime
hard work in his medium, and a capacity to feel at least as
strongly about his medium as about his subject.

In any art form, feeling must be translated into equiva-
lents. Not feeling itself, but feeling translated into themes
that enrich one another with the medium. You, sir, are human and feel things, but you have no responsive feeling for
the medium and are, therefore, no poet.

Do I offend you? I mean only to prick you out of every
person's ego illusions into a useful introspection. You have
tried for major utterance, have you? Let's assume instead I
am your Freshman English teacher and am red penciling a
theme you have written. Would I offend you if I red-lined
the following phrases and margined them as "tr" for "trite?"

> spinning void
> aching loneliness
> far reaches of outer space (I'm damned if I know of
>   any near reaches out there.)
> echoing infinities (do they echo?)
> the confines of my heart
> eternal verities unparsed
> a love forever new

I don't doubt that you have taken your new fatherhood
intensely. It is language—to cite your prime failure—that
you have belittled. Do you really imagine that such shop-
worn, puffed-up phrases are the language in which poetry
can reach the power of human feeling?

Bless the birth and the house of the birth. I'll risk your
dislike if I can make you see you have squandered good feeling on language that isn't good enough for what you are
feeling.

But having been honest at your expense let me be honest at my own. By now, I confess, I am no longer writing to you, though I do rejoice with you at the life that starts here. Somewhere along the line I began to write not to your questions but to the same questions asked over and over again in the letters that accompany poems to my desk at the *Saturday Review*.

Bad poetry, I have to believe, follows bad listening. How can anyone have listened to the sounds an English poem makes from *Beowulf* to Auden and then have settled for metronomic clichés as a full equivalent of deeply felt experiences? It can't be done, not even by an ego. The writers of such poems are not bad listeners, they are non-listeners. They haven't read—not in joy. They have never listened to an orchestra in full passion. How else could they assume that an ocarina makes music?

And so you all see, you have a right to feel offended. I have refused you the praise you wanted. And, worse, I have turned your personal question into a column aimed at defending my desk from the sort of questions other people ask me many times a day. Their questions are always the same as yours. They all assume, without benefit of acquaintance, that an editor is a teacher.

All I can plead toward an inadequate defense is that I could not have afforded the time to discuss your poem at length unless I could turn the discussion into something that might serve my need, too. If that is selfish, no writer has anything to offer his readers but their own selfish pleasure in reading what he writes, if he can make it a selfish pleasure for them. If he cannot, he fails—at least for that reader. To succeed, he must first find his own selfish pleasure in writing what he does in the way he does.

Take selfishness as a workable bond. At the distance imposed by any medium, selfishness, whenever reader and writer can join in it, becomes pleasure exchanged—as one can go selfishly to Virgil's self-pleasure in the writing, the child, the father, the poet, and a long succession of critics, all long dead.

But first long life to this father, to this child, and to the mother.

Yours,
John Ciardi

"Juvenile Poetry"
and Poetry for Children

I WANT to have some fun and talk about what is usually called "juvenile poetry." My editor at Lippincott got so tired of being referred to as the "juvenile editor" that she began to call all the other editors "senile editors." I have been asked how I began writing children's poems, and whether I gear them to the children. I don't know any of the rules of children's poetry. When I was teaching at Harvard, I lived in the same house with my sister. She had some children that were small, and I wrote some poems for them. They grew up and got to be large oafs uninterested in poetry, so I stopped it for a while. Then my own children came along and I began to write some more. I had quite a stack of them somewhere, but I had never thought of publishing children's poems until one day Eunice Blake said, "You ought to write some children's poems." I told her I had a ten-year-old file folder full of the things and she said, "Send it to me." She sent me two contracts for my first two books out of this old folder, and that was the beginning of it.

I have been asked if I write for my children. I used to, but they are more interested in the Beatles and various other things right now. Also they are in a terrible hurry to grow up, and I am not. That gives me a lot more time than they have. Their attention span is about seven seconds and mine is at least fifteen, which gives me that much advantage over them. I think I am writing for the child in me. I hope to make my childhood last longer than theirs. They are in a hurry to get out of it, and I'm trying to hold on to it. I have had some interesting experiences in the business of writing children's poems, and some of them are related to the school system.

When my daughter was just entering kindergarten, Houghton Mifflin, for whom I had done a textbook, asked me to do a book using a simplified first grade vocabulary. I said it sounded like fun, but I didn't know anything about it. They said they would give me the vocabulary that I had to use. They gave me a sheet with the 420-word vocabulary that first graders are responsible for. This is the minimum requirement for the first grade to cover by the end of the year. Right now there seems to be a revulsion against that sort of book, but I disagree. It is Pablum in a sense, and yet there is a point in the organism when Pablum is the natural food. The thing to do with Pablum is not to outlaw it but to get over it as fast as possible and go on to steak.

English is a very difficult language for children to learn. It has a complicated phonetic code. English-speaking children are slow to learn to read as compared to Italian children because Italian has a simple phonetic code. In Italian, everything is pronounced exactly as it is spelled and every letter always has the same pronunciation. There are perhaps six or seven rules that count; no exceptions. Now think how many ways an English-speaking child has to carry in mind to pronounce an E.

The only point of the simplified vocabulary is to try to give the beginner some assurance on the page. If you are teaching the child that *by* spells "by," you should wait a little while before you run in "*buy.*" Since you are trying to begin him on vowel sounds, you stay away from most of the dipthongs. The list I was given did not have *ai* on it. It had *ea,* as in wheat, and bread, to get them used to this exception, but not *ai.* I wanted to say rain in one poem, but I couldn't use the word rain. I walked the floor and kicked the cat and abused my wife all one afternoon, trying to find a way around the word rain. Finally there came to me what I think was an improvement. I said, "The water came down like strings of wet."

The advantage of any limitation is that it forces you around, which sometimes gives you a better way out than you would have had if there had been no resistance. You want something a little harder than you can quite manage because it is such a thrill to manage it. Every limitation of this sort is valuable. I certainly do not insist that the first grade vocabulary should stay forever, and I think poems should introduce one or two new words. Nothing is damaged if the child has to run to mother or to the teacher and say, "What is this word?" as long as he has thirty known words surrounding it on each side. They give the beginner a foothold on the page, so that he can feel at home at it.

Later I tried another idea. Bedtime reading should be a two-way street I think. I did a book called *You Read to Me and I'll Read to You* in which I shuffled the poems and printed them in two colors of ink. There were simplified poems for the child to read to the adult alternating with poems of an unlimited vocabulary for the adult to read back to the child.

I began with this simplified vocabulary and did a book called *I Met a Man* with a special purpose. My daughter was in kindergarten then, and I wanted to write the first book she read all the way through. I achieved this ambition.

While she was in kindergarten she had this book in a black folder she carried around under her arm. She would walk along the street like the Ancient Mariner stopping people, and they had a poem read to them whether they liked it or not. There were a number of riddle games, too. A riddle is a natural way of working in a new word. The child can guess the answer and then see it written.

Since I began to work on a first grade vocabulary, I learned something else. As I read non-juvenile poetry, so many passages of enduring poetry turn out to be written very close to a first grade vocabulary. It isn't the words, it is the complexity of the thought that would baffle a child. For example there is a very complex line by Robert Frost, "Back out of all this now too much for us." Every word is a first grade word, but it is no first grade thought. It is a very daring line. Only a master would risk it and keep that simplicity. Any number of his poems run to practically this simplified vocabulary.

> The people along the sand
> They all look out one way.
> They turn their backs on the land
> They all look out at the bay.

That is no child's poem, but "people" is the one word in there that isn't on the first grade vocabulary. No bright child halfway through the first grade would have any trouble with the word "people." That is Robert Frost writing a serious poem, and yet the words of it, one by one, are practically first grade vocabulary words.

I don't know what any of you got out of the genetic grab-bag, but I did not get angel fluffs. I got young savages. They are acquisitive, noisy, angry, competitive, lovable when you can stand them, but nevertheless young savages. I didn't see any way of getting my children sugar-coated, but

78

I wanted to engage them, so I wrote poems that were natural to them and natural to me. It seems that the language of childhood, the imagination of childhood, is naturally violent. I don't like Anderson's fairy tales. I think Grimm does a much better job with the psyche. The child says, "Read us the one about the birds that pecked out the bad sister's eyes!"

The genteel assumption, which is really a Platonic assumption, seems to be that if children read about birds pecking out a bad sister's eyes, they will go out and peck bad sister's eyes. I think that is nonsense. In the first place, children have a firm sense of the difference between real and pretend. When they lose this difference they are sick. They belong in the hands of a counselor, psychologist, or psychiatrist. Any healthy child knows the difference between real and pretend violence. It is an assurance, I think, to see these violent things put into form and made into a dance and a pleasure. I think it is a therapy.

Plato was a very primitive critic. He believed that we become that which we contemplate. Therefore, he put the poets out of his republic because he said that poets should hold up to us examples of virtue. Virtue is rather dull to write about and he recognized that. He knew it is natural for poets to write about vice and violence, but he didn't want the citizens of his republic to be contemplating vice and violence. Therefore, he wanted to send away all the poets except a few to be kept around to write battle hymns. That is sanctified violence.

Criticism remained in that primitive state until Aristotle came along and sophisticated it with the idea of vicarious experience. That is implicit in his theory of tragedy—that you identify only formally with the character within a formal action. This involves your emotions and, by a process of catharsis, works them out for you vicariously. You come out resolved and calm. That is the difference between primitive and sophisticated criticism. In one sense, we went from the dawn age to the present time when we went from Plato to Aristotle. Yet as far as children are concerned, we are still being Platonic in our view of what they can and cannot take. I think Aristotle was much more the perceptive man.

There is such a thing as vicarious experience. You can live out your violences, your feelings, within form. Because form is a happy thing, these impulses are given a happy release rather than a frustrating inhibition. Certainly there are ways of perverting that argument, but I dislike the notion that if children have a good time with their natural impulses, somehow they are not being civilized.

I wrote this book of first grade poems for my own young savages, Houghton Mifflin published it, and then they had trouble. They wanted to sell the book to the school system, and the school system wouldn't take it. They said, "We can't ask children to read those poems." This made me hope that maybe I was on the right track when they started referring to them as "those poems." Houghton Mifflin had me locked up with a man who said he represented the school system, but I think what he represented was a catastrophe on its way downhill.

He began to object to all the poems I seemed to like best. He took off on one which was a triple-rhyming thing.

> I met a man who lived in a house
> With a cat, and a dog, a bird and a mouse
> And a big gold fish, and a little brown louse.

I told him it was on the list I had been given, but he said, "We don't encourage it." I tried another argument. W. H. Auden once said that English is the language in which doom rhymes with womb. You have to write pessimistic poetry. If you start with womb, where can you go? Room,

broom, zoom, then loom, doom, and tomb rhyme, but that
is about it. You have no choice. If you start with womb, you
must end up with the looming doom of the tomb. That is
the way English goes.

How many rhymes are there when you start with house
and mouse? Where do you go from there? I could have said
blouse, but there is no context for it. Spouse is a little silly in
this thing. I could have said souse, and that would probably
identify Daddy well enough, but there aren't many places to
go. I wanted to say that semantically words have denotation and connotations. Children use the word "louse" without denotation. It is simply a noise you make at your sister
when you are not pleased with her. It has no reference, it
just has a flavor. Isn't it educational to have children know
that there is a little animal called a louse? They don't see
many of them in this day of DDT and sanitation. None of
this would do. He objected to "louse."

Then he came down on another poem I was very happy
about.

> I met a man that was trying to whittle
> A ship from a stick, but little by little
> The ship he whittled grew littler and littler
> Said he with a sigh, "I'm a very bad whittler!
> I've whittled my ship till it's small as a boat.
> Then I whittled a hole in it—how will it float?"
> So he threw it away and cut his throat.

That was the way it was published in the first edition of
the book, and I submit there is not much else you can do in
that situation. The man from the school system objected to
it. He said something about archetypal behavior patterns. I
wondered if he meant children would all buy switchblades
and go out cutting one another's throats. He went into another discussion of optimum archetypal behavioral pat-

terns. He was very good at it. As I listened to him in admiration, I had an idea. A light had just gone on in my head, and in the second edition this couplet is added.

> And when he saw his head was gone
> He whittled another and put that on.

That makes a happy ending. I don't see anything in that to damage a little psyche. Why is it any worse than this?

> There was a man in our town.
> And he was wondrous wise,
> He jumped into the bramble bush
> And scratched out both his eyes.
> And when he saw his eyes were out
> With all his might and main,
> He jumped into another bush,
> And scratched them in again.

I love that little poem. I think it's one of the best of those of Mother Goose. There is violence in it, but what difference does it make? It is not violent violence. It is play violence, dance violence, like "Bang! Bang! You're dead!" Nations seem to go through a blood bath of guilt. When one crazy man in Dallas shot the president, there were serious proposals that children be brought to the town square to dump all their toy guns in a bonfire. It would be not a book-burning, but a plastic gun-burning. What is going to keep them from going "Bang! Bang!" with their fingers? I think the fact is something else. Children will always play at what the tribe does for a living. So long as we are a warlike nation, the children will play "Bang! Bang! You're Dead!" As long as their brothers are in the army and the newsreels and TV are full of soldiers, they will do what the tribe does. In a fishing tribe the children play at being fishers, in a weaving tribe the children play at being weavers. We are a military

tribe and the children are going to play "Bang! Bang!" because that is what the tribe is doing.

The man from the school system objected to a poem that
was a pure exercise in matching sounds. I got to playing
with, "The cat heard, the cat bird" . . . how many combinations of sound can you make? I wanted this to be written in first grade vocabulary so I began:

> One day, a fine day, a high-flying-sky day
> A cat-bird, a fat bird, a fine fat cat bird
> Was sitting and singing on a stump by the highway
> Just sitting. And singing. Just that. But a cat heard.
>
> A thin cat, a grin-cat, a long, thin grin-cat
> Came creeping the sly way by the highway to the
>   stump.
> "O cat-bird, the cat heard! O cat-bird, scat!
> The grin-cat is creeping! He is going to jump!"
>
> One day, a fine day, a high-flying-sky day
> A fat cat, yes that cat we met as a thin cat
> Was napping, cat-napping on a stump by the
>   highway,
> And even in his sleep you could see he was a
>   grin-cat.
>
> Why was he grinning? He must have had a dream
> What made him fat? a pan full of cream
> What about the cat-bird? what bird, dear?
> I don't see any cat-bird here.

Somehow, I was told, that was offensive to small psyches. He suggested that maybe we shouldn't tell children
this early that cats eat birds. We should leave them un-
prepared, or un-upset, or whatever it was. We argued that
back and forth.

83

I had written a simple little double limerick that I was happy about. There were two limericks in a row making the poem. Children have an absorption with bugs, and little crawling things. I tried to catch some of that in this poem. He didn't like it.

> I said to a bug in the sink
> "Are you taking a swim or a drink?"
>   "I", said the bug,
>   "Am a sea-going tug,
> Am I headed for land do you think?"
> "What a silly," I said, "that's no sea
> It's a sink." — "A sink it may be
>   But I'd sooner I think
>   Be at sea in the sink
> Than a sink in the sea, sir," said he.

It was just play, but his objection stopped me cold. He said, "It makes the American home sound unsanitary." He reminded me of that man's wife coming in from the kitchen saying, "What goes on here?" I knew my own law; there was no more talk to be had with him. But that was all right, and perhaps as it should be. My poems were for the children.

On Writing and Bad Writing

"How do I learn to write?" It is almost certain (perhaps not quite) that anyone who insists upon asking it that way will never find the answer. It is a naive question. But perhaps it is good for honest people to be badgered by the innocent, ignorant, and yet primary question. If confusion follows, praise all that sends honest people honestly to their confusions.

No one who writes seriously, and by seriously I mean as a way of life, will write in any but his own way. His way of life is, in fact, to find just his own way of writing—whatever way most nearly informs for him the emotions of experiencing this world.

A good writing coach should be able to teach a bright student to write almost like Dickens, or almost like Donne, or almost like Emerson. Any number of surfaces can reflect fire. The starting need of the writer is to be himself the tinder.

If he is that tinder, any library is full of sparks, and almost any teacher could be Prometheus.

But how does the would-be writer begin?

The first answer is easy: Because he is a human being and because he is sensitive to the joy and distress of that condition, he is moved to speak his feelings. He begins there.

But that is not enough. If human passion is first, it must yet be joined by an equal passion for the medium before good writing can happen. The writer is a person overpowered by words, sentences, rhythms, ideas, the drama of ideas when there are lives moving in them, and the forms a writer can shape from the medium. Language haunts the writer. Words, sentences, rhythms are not things to the writer; they are presences. The presence of his medium makes him feel more than he really knows how to think or say. He knows that he is wiser, richer, more perceptive, more sentient when he is immersed in his medium than he can hope to be when he is high and dry in ideas and presences that he can identify and talk about with clear and pedagogical coherence. His medium is a gorgeous confusion upon him and a flowering of all possibility. It is his house of great ghosts.

No teacher can hope to build for the student that haunted house of the mortally excited talent and self, but the good teacher recognizes the excitement when it appears and can encourage it as one encourages a fire by poking, prodding, and blowing on it. But it is dangerous to think that the fire is the teacher's doing. At best, the teacher may strike the match.

One of the troubles with beginning writers is that they are almost certain to blaze out of control. Often it is the teacher's job to squirt a little water here and there. For the object is to heat and to illuminate the house, not to burn it down. The act of distinguishing between the logs of the fireplace and the walls of the house is called criticism, and I am tempted to claim that any fires that have been put out as a result of the act of criticism should never have been started.

Writing involves containment. Like all art, it takes place within limits. If writing is thought of as the fire of the soul— and let this be the end of the incendiary metaphor—it must remain within the iron limits of the grate. If it is thought of as happening within a frame, the frame may be hacked at by a true genius (and only by a true genius), but it must not be broken by any writer. Writing, like all art, is a formality. The writing cannot be made to take the place of the world. The world will remain in its own sprawl.

Whatever we mean by reality, writing is not it. Writing selects from the unknown reality of things, and, by selecting, makes known. Writing is a heightening, an ordering, perhaps only a moment's ordering; whatever it is, it remains that glimpse through a frame that no one may live in but that the best must live toward. Art has no other function.

What then? What does one tell would-be writers? Granting that there are no certainties, that all must be groped for, that there is no teaching of writing but only the coaching one can give to self-learners—is there no useful generalization?

I am inclined to offer one above all others, and that is that the badness of bad writing is never visible to the writer. I offer that as a generalization and not as a truth, for it is not always but only sometimes true.

Conceivably one could try to write with all mortal passion, and write badly, and still retain enough taste and detachment to know that he is writing badly. In the exhaustions of honesty, such a person invariably gives up the effort, finds some way of making a living and, having found a living, probably becomes an excellent reader, made the more sensitive to the writing by his own sad sense of failure; as perhaps a man of exquisite ear but badly coordinated muscles may have dreamed of playing the cello but could never make his arms and fingers produce what his ear dreamed of hearing. Such people, however, are rare, for it takes a person of rare taste to recognize failure against all the promptings of the ego that allow the tasteless to go on producing and cherishing stuff.

My generalization is likely to be untrue of hopeful writers on their way to being good writers. A writer can, in fact, develop only as rapidly as he learns to recognize what is bad in his writing. If a man means his writing seriously he must mean to write well. But how can he write well until he learns to see what he has written badly? His progress toward good writing and his recognition of bad writing are bound to unfold at something like the same rate. Give me the young writer who is ashamed this week of what he wrote last week, and I will take him as my example of hope.

Anyone can write a bad story or a bad poem. Having written it, one may stay in love with it forever, and another burn it in anguish. Where can hope be, in this case, but with the arsonist? Whether or not he can itemize the causes of the badness, he has learned that it is bad. All human chance is that he will not fall back into that particular kind of badness, or at least not for long.

As poetry editor of the *Saturday Review*, I systematically refused to enter into personal criticism of manuscripts submitted unless I was seriously considering them for publication. I refused for many reasons, including the statistical one that I received more such requests in a week than I could honor in a year. But the reason above all others is that in practically all cases such criticism would be pointless. I think I could identify the badness of most of the poems submitted, but bad writers will not see the badness of their own writing even when it's pointed out. There are, heaven knows, understandable human reasons for that blindness. Even bad writing is likely to be powered by intense emotion. Feeling so moved, the bad writer is easily self-persuaded to take the power of the starting emotion as a measure of the writing. Consequently he sees only what was intended, never what was written.

Such a one is the entirely hopeless writer, who is usually given to assaults upon the largest possible subjects. In mildest moments, he is satisfied with stating the ultimate truth about childhood, grandma, the flag, and love. In full flight, he settles for nothing less than nature's inner meaning and the intentions of the universe. He does not see the writing because, in plain fact, he cares nothing about it. He is out for release, not for containment. He is a self-expresser, not a maker.

Usually such a writer will defend himself fiercely against all criticism. We might wonder why he even asks for it, except that we already know that it wasn't criticism, but praise, he came for. Whichever it is, you simply avoid giving it.

The hopeful writer may beg off because he is already ashamed of what he passed in for criticism. If he does want the criticism, he will see the point of most of it at once. The most hopeful response I know is that of the writer who says, "You're probably right, but let me take that away to think about. I need time to feel it out."

That is the most hopeful response because such a writer, even as a beginner, has learned how multiple writing is, how many auras must be registered in arriving at his own sense of the light, and because no criticism is really to his purpose until he has registered it upon his own sense of the light.

That writer is going back to look at the writing and to think about it. And may, I suspect, manage to see it. He is not simply taking criticism, he is receiving it. And each perception so received is being built into him—wired into him, so to speak, as one more circuit of sensitivity in the infinite complex of the nervous system. The next time he writes, he will have one more awareness going for him.

In time, that complex conditioning, those millions of

awarenesses wired into his dendrites, will generate something almost separate from him. Critics call that something "aesthetic distance" or "detachment." Whatever it is called, it identifies a central possession of every good writer—the ability to be passionately committed to what he is writing at the same time that awareness is detached, calculating, and technical.

That state is neither easily achieved nor easily defined, but it comes close to being a first condition of all good writing, with an exception to be made only for those rare impassioned moments when a genius—which is to say a writer who has disciplined himself without losing the wildness of his talents—pours out, say, a "Kubla Khan" in a moment of what seems to be blind rapture. Is it necessary to argue that even a Coleridge must have the discipline and essential duplicities of a lifetime to draw upon to give form to his moment of rapture? This world's writing is put on its page by those who have developed their talents to a point of doubleness that lets them be passionately in the writing at the same time that their monitoring awareness as artists are out of it.

Those awarenesses begin exactly in the writer's ability to see what has been written, in the ability to get outside the writing, to become its reader as well as its writer, and to learn from it.

Liberal Arts and the Arts

ALTHOUGH I taught school for about twenty years, I always felt divided within myself when I tried to teach poetry, partly because the academic procedure is necessarily a rational one, while a poem has to be a passion or it is nothing. For years I have been fumbling for the terms of that conflict.

I think I came upon an answer one day when I found myself on a panel with a distinguished colleague of mine, the dean of an Engineering School, a man for whom I have a great deal of respect. It was one of those panels systematically convoked in academia and infallibly given impossible titles. This one was called Creative Thinking.

Our little group of serious thinkers sat there, each stroking his metaphorical beard and being creative about thinking, then I heard the dean rise and say something that frightened me. He said, "There are five steps to creative thinking."

I am afraid of that sort of mind.

My last year at Rutgers I taught graduate seminars for teachers looking for master's degrees in education and English. The questions the teachers would throw at me were on that order. They would say, "What are the twelve aims of education?" I think they took a course in philosophy of education somewhere and the professor walked in with his own problems and said something to the effect that "We can't spend all the hours of every day splitting hairs; therefore, for the purposes of this course I am going to discuss the material under twelve headings and we will call each one an 'aim.'" This is a matter of convenience.

But what the class heard was, "There are twelve aims of education" and down came the curtain. Everything was divided into twelve boxes and everything had to fit into those boxes. If it didn't fit, you made it fit, and if there was a little too much, you whopped something off and threw it away.

This is the categorical mind at work, and I was afraid I had run into another example of it. When one does, it's the end of discussion. You have to change the subject or get out of there.

Then the dean went on to name his five steps: (1) Define the limits of your problem; (2) Undertake the necessary qualitative analysis; (3) Perform the quantitative mathematics required by your qualitative analysis; (4)(a very prudent step) Check your mathematics; and (5) Find the mechanical implementation of your mathematical solution.

By the time he was through, I found that I disagreed only with his label and didn't have any real argument with him. The contents were sound enough; he was describing a valuable process and one that is deeply involved in one of the sub-species of education. It was not, however, creative thinking—it was problem solving.

Now problem solving is a very respectable, desirable, and necessary approach to dealing with matter. I live in New

Jersey and I commute into New York from time to time through one of the tunnels or across the George Washington Bridge, and I like to feel when I'm in the middle of the bridge that the problems met in building it were solved by someone who was good at it. So I have no quarrel whatever with problem solvers. It's part of what we do. But it isn't all of what we do.

The difference might be put in these terms: I don't think it's possible to do any of the essential, one might say the cardinal, things of life in terms of these five steps. (Cardinal is the right word, for it comes from the Latin *cardus*, meaning "hinge"; that is, the turning point.) You can't get married that way, you can't beget a child that way. I don't think you can die decently that way. Whatever happens of major consequence in your life is beyond these five steps.

I don't think a boy can pick out a girl and define her limits and undertake a qualitative analysis and then perform some mathematics and check it out and find the mechanical implementation. Now and then, I have run into a couple that made me think that might have been the way it happened. But it's not the warmest family atmosphere. I don't like to think about it too long. I would rather be somewhere else after a while.

Certain irrationalities are of our essence. We try to discipline the human mind. It is necessary, but all of us, if we are honest, have to admit that we do crazy things on purpose, and if we get that far in the admission, we will sometimes confess that we behave this way most of the time. Aldous Huxley speaks of the "endless idiot gibberish of the reverie." Take your attention off your mind, and an ape starts shaking the tree of nerves that you live in.

I would like to defend the arts in terms of their essential and committed irrationalities. We have to go deeper into ourselves than the faces we prepare to meet the faces that we meet, as Eliot more or less put it. Our social encounters are in those terms, but poetry, like all of the arts, has to whisper deeper.

Let me digress now, or seem to digress. We will come back to where we are.

A university is a reading and discussion club. If students knew how to use the library, they wouldn't need the rest of the buildings. The faculty's job, in great part, is to teach students how to use a library in a living way. All a student should really need is access to the library and a place to sleep.

Some of the European universities come close to doing this. One can go to lectures or not, but primarily one undertakes a reading program, calling on one's tutorial person at least once a week to exchange opinions.

Another thing the faculty does is offer specimens of how various kinds of minds trained in various kinds of disciplines work. It is interesting to find the connections that a well-trained economist will make. It is interesting to see what connections a person well-trained in music will make—or in literature or in philosophy or psychology or sociology.

By the time you have some samples of how a disciplined mind works, and can take them into your reading, you are doing well. The duty of a liberal arts college lies in transmitting that information from one generation to the next.

That information—those samples—are of two kinds. Mankind has been finding out a lot about matter, about its environment, about that body of news we call "science." But mankind has also been trying out the experiences of being alive on this planet and what it comes to, and we call that body of news "the humanities."

It is not a matter of being told about Job or Aida, about Oedipus or Medea, about Ulysses or Dante. It is a matter of reliving their experiences. Just as a beginning scientist needs to go back and perform experiments that scientists of the past have performed, just so and even more so, we need to go back and relive the experience of Job on his dung heap, to find ourselves there, understanding how it feels to suffer this loss, how it feels to get into the vast questions that Job is caught up in.

I am talking now about the difference between experiencing a thing and being told a thing. Suppose an actor, billed to do a performance of Hamlet, had decided to bring down the curtain and step forward and say, "Ladies and gentlemen, I'm a little tired today. I don't want to act out this scene—it's rather arduous. Instead, let me tell you about it." He would have cheated you.

And you should have thrown rotten eggs. It is a duty, as one loves the theatre, to resist pedantry as a substitute for performance. You came for an experience, not for a lecture.

And all of art is experience. It is deeply involved in a double process that begins for me with something that Emerson said. "It is the 'not me' in my friend that delights me." I think that is the first expansion—to find pleasure in the kind of perception that is not yours.

How this process proceeds can be very simply seen. All of our colleges have a weekly ritual called the "theme," sometimes with a capital "T" and sometimes in the lower case "t," but week after week, freshmen perform this dark ritual. I used to watch my students put down a mindless sentence and then in the right margin of the page write "17." Then they would write more and put down another number and, bit by bit, were creeping up on the magic thousand words. They didn't much care what they were writing, so long as the words were adding up to a thousand.

✓The freshman theme, expository writing in general, the academic paper, is organized paragraph by paragraph. It's a form of problem solving. The process of trying to teach freshmen to write is basically an exercise in logic. It is legal training. The teaching of paragraph structure consists largely in bringing a student to make an intelligent definition or an

95

intelligent generalization. What is the topic sentence, the topic assertion? Is it reasonably stated? Is the paragraph well contained? Does it make sense as a term in a logical process?

An expository paragraph is an exercise in evidence. How much evidence is needed to support the generalization that was made? In what order should that evidence be presented? Is there too much of it? All of these questions are more or less mechanically teachable.

But creative writing, if that is the word for it, goes by another process. Fiction is written not paragraph by paragraph but scene by scene. And the point of going scene by scene is quite simple, if you begin to look at the nature of the scene. We could say the same thing about a painting, a piece of music, a poem, but it becomes most visible in terms of fiction; so let me address it in those terms.

A scene in fiction, as soon as it's isolated, can be observed to have rhythm, pace, climax, and a number of characteristics, but above all, it has one character to whose interior workings you as the reader have access. That character is your means of perception, the person you are to become for the purpose, for the moment, of the scene. He is the "not me" with whom you identify by the process of empathy.

There is nothing new to us about the process of empathy. When I was small and went to the Saturday afternoon movies, when the hero came in, I would empathize to the top of my lungs. We know with whom we are to identify—who it is we are to become.

I began going to these movies, I guess, about 1923 or 1924. That was something like six years after the last of *The Perils of Pauline*, the cliff-hanger serials, were made, but they were still showing every Saturday. We used to discuss all week what might happen next week, and on Saturdays we would race to the movies to find out.

No matter what terrible plight Pauline was in, she always

escaped. She ripped her dress slightly and escaped. It got to be a little anthology of rips as the scene progressed. She would escape from a gorilla, who was about to strangle her, and duck into a castle to bump into a skeleton or a cobweb or something that would frighten her, and she would cower backwards against the wall. Then a sliding door would open, a great hairy arm would reach out from the wall, and everyone would shout, "Look Out!"

Nobody, nobody, ever, ever said, "Get her, Hairy Arm!"

As a matter of fact, I had *The Perils of Pauline* come to my mind years later when I was a fan of Charles Addams, because his whole humor is the act of cheering for Hairy Arm. And I could rewrite that story so that we would all cheer for the Hairy Arm. Because there's a little bit of Hairy Arm in all of us.

There is this poor orphan Hairy Arm. He is sealed into the walls of the castle, by, let us say, some sort of spell. He walks back and forth inside these castle walls. He looks out through chinks, and here and there across the landscape he sees a blonde in a slightly torn dress racing about, and he wants one. But every time he has prepared himself to reach for her everybody shouts "look out" and the object moves out of range. He must pull out and go back into his dank castle walls.

The point I am trying to make is what Emerson said: it is the "not me" in my friend that delights me. The next step, and the true liberalizing process, is the discovery that there is no "not me"—that you can identify with anything human and find that you are like it. You can identify with Pauline one time, and with the Hairy Arm another, and you will find that you are partly Pauline and partly Hairy Arm. You can identify with the cops or the robbers, depending on how a story is told. In so doing, you are trying on a human experience.

You can pick up a book and a voice says, "Call me Ishmael," and you find yourself north of New Bedford on a blowy night with a man who has been teaching school so long that he needs a whaling trip. To get fresh wind through his mind he has left the classroom and he's leisurely walking down to New Bedford to go to sea.

I found myself walking down that road with him. We got to New Bedford and checked in at a local grog shop, an inn, and I asked for a room and I found I had to share the bed with some harpooner. I wasn't told who he was. I woke up in the middle of the night and found a tattooed savage performing some dark ritual by the fire. I covered my eyes and went back to bed and woke up in the morning and found the man's arm across me; I didn't dare move. But we became friends, and we signed up on a ship called the *Pequod* with some strange Quaker owners who wouldn't give me much of a share, but they gave him a big share because he was experienced. I was a greenhorn. Four years later I found myself floating on a coffin in the South Pacific. This happened to me.

I spent four years in the army and I think I can't say, now that both are over, that my four years on the *Pequod* were less real than my four years in the army. If anything, my four years on the *Pequod* were contained in a better imagination. It had a better pattern to it. It came to better purposes. I think I met better people when I was sailing on the *Pequod,* although there is a certain resemblance between Captain Ahab and some of the people I met in the army. This is experience.

There is not time in one lifetime to acquire all the experiences you have to acquire and to meet all the people you have to meet, if you mean to be a developed and civilized human being. You can't do it except in imagination. That's why I understood E. E. Cumings when he was asked the question, "What about the world, Mr. Cummings?", and he said, "I live in so many; which one?"

Now, short of the point at which you lose contact and cannot find relation within yourself, that's necessary—you have to live in different worlds.

There is sometimes wisdom in jargon. Teachers today never speak of an "underprivileged child." They say rather, "a child whose experiences have been limited to his immediate environment." That starts to be jargon, but I think it comes out to be a piece of wisdom. Intellectually, artistically, and socially, in terms of civilization, that is what it means to be underprivileged. If your experiences are limited to your immediate environment, you are living in a thin and shallow universe. Where in your immediate environment are you going to meet Dante or Shakespeare? There isn't one on your block, unless you happen to live next to the library.

This is the function of the liberal arts. Part of it is irrational. I can't think of anything to tell the censor if he says, "So you think *Moby Dick* is a pretty good book. Well, what do you think about that scene where we're shown a naked savage prostrate before a little idol that he carries around with him? Do you think that's socially useful?"

I can't say that it's socially useful. I think it is humanly useful to get into every human environment there is. But hardly a week goes by without an effort by someone to close a border into another place. Baudelaire was taken to court and was ordered to remove some poems from his book. Parents' groups in school systems all over America, even today, are on the lookout for naked savages.

Actually, I think of Baudelaire as a saintly man. There isn't a trace of obscenity in him. But the literal mind, the categorical mind, the problem-solving mind, unless it is broadened by the humanities, is always closing the border.

I do like the mind that can solve problems, but our real problems are human. They concern how profoundly we manage to experience ourselves, and how truly we manage to get out of our tight, immediate environment into that conceptual neighborhood where you hold discourse with Aristotle, Plato, Plotinus, Homer, Dante, Shakespeare, Augustus, Sophocles, and all the names we use when we mean the Western mind.

The Student Poet

L ET a discussion begin with an assumption that no one writes immortal poems in his student days. A student poet may do relatively brilliant work, but if five years out of college he still likes what he wrote before graduation, that fact may in itself be taken as evidence that he will not amount to anything as a poet. What good violinist, for example, listening to a tape of his own playing five years ago when he was still in the conservatory, can allow himself to be satisfied with it?

Student work is not an end in itself. It is valuable only as it teaches the student to do better. In the arts the student will do better only as he is willing to accept the difficulty of working within fixed disciplines. In poetry, the fixed disciplines are rhyme, metrics, and form. No matter that the student handles those formal elements badly: the point is that he must try to handle them, for only as he tries to overcome those difficulties can he learn his craft.

Obviously, free verse offers him no such opportunity to learn. Out with it. Students will insist on writing it, and the editors of undergraduate magazines cannot always reject all of it, but the teacher of writing has no business encouraging such stuff. Let the student's soul be ever so sensitive, the teacher must stand firm. "If you will not take the trouble to put it into form," he is well advised to tell the student, "I will not take the trouble to read it."

An accomplished writer may venture into free verse when he is sufficiently sure of himself, but no student can permit himself such assurance. For the student seems to think that free verse is easy to write. It is only easy to write badly. To write free verse well (and it can be written well) requires such control that the poet can improvise his form as he goes. What the free-versifiers in the student body never know is that there really is no such thing as free verse: all poetry must have form, and until a poet has mastered the traditional forms he is not qualified to try more elusive measures. The reader is under no compulsion to take seriously any fellow student's free verse.

For unless the poet strives to give form to his experience, he is not writing a poem at all, but only self-expressing. Such self-expression may have high therapeutic value, and it may be strongly recommended by the family psychiatrist, but poetry is not simply an outpouring: it is a pouring-into, and what it is poured into is form.

Everyone commits this sort of self-expression at one time or another. Usually it goes for ecstasy:

> I'm dreaming of you
> Night after night after night . . .
> Dreams . . .
>   Oh, God
> Nothing but dreams. . . !

This may be such stuff as the churn of adolescent glands is made of, but it is obviously not poetry, and no one should encourage it.

If the student poet escapes this sort of formless cry, he still has many levels of badness to rise through. Apart from the problems in premature free verse, perhaps the principal weakness of bad poetry is that it starts too large. The reader would do well to watch the first lines of a poem. What sort of opening statement has the would-be poet committed? Here, for example, are a number of opening lines so inflated that the best of poets could not hope to write a poem sustaining the claim they make:

> Life is beauty ever dawning
> *or*
> My soul is boundless as the sea
> *or*
> Truth is a gull's wing in the sky
> *or*
> You taught me all a heart can hold

Or consider the following couplet:

> I held a shell against my ear
> And heard the voice of God ring clear.

What could any man possibly write that would be meaningfully the voice of God in that shell? Even ignoring the fact that the sound in a sea shell does not exactly "ring clear," what could God be represented as saying? The poem is foredoomed to grow larger and sillier.

"Leave some of the universe for the next poem," one is tempted to say. "Don't try to force it all into sixteen lines." The larger the statement, moreover, the more likely it is to become nonsense. A statement that fails to make sense in prose is not automatically elevated to sublimity by being set as verse.

One of the most reliable formulas for poetry—one that may be observed in every language and tradition of poetry—is the movement from the specific and small to the general and large. The student is well advised to open his poem with the most precise statement he can manage about the most carefully observed specific detail he can locate. Let him shun all trace of greater significance. Let him concentrate on making some specific thing, scene, or action as vivid as possible. His opening concern is to describe; only that. By the time he has completed his description—especially if he is word-sensitive—something else will have happened. The words he chose for their descriptive accuracy will have accumulated as a series of connotations. They will have released a ghost of second suggestion, a ghost he did not have in mind when he began. And once that opening description has been firmed and the ghost released, the poem to come is between the poet and that ghost. The poet does not know where he is going, but he knows when he has arrived. He follows the poem into itself, as a composer follows his theme into itself. But neither poet nor musician can begin to follow until something has been started. It is important for that "something" to be as specific and as vivid as possible.

And the poet can learn early to stand back and look at the poem. He might begin his assessment of it by noting how soon he lets the reader know where he stands. How far into the poem must one go before he has been shown an object? an action? before he feels that he has located the scene?

Having located the opening specification the reader should then follow through: How does the poem develop to its larger meaning? How much ground has been covered between the beginning and the end? Has the movement from small to large been natural and unstrained? Does the larger implication truly develop from the opening specification? Could the poet have covered the same (emotional) ground in fewer lines?

There is another kind of weakness, for which these questions offer little help: this is the weakness that results from imitation. Students sometimes become excellent imitators of their chosen masters. The trouble is most likely to be that the student does not know he is imitating. He thinks *he* is the author of his poem, when in fact he has borrowed it almost bodily.

It seems obvious that the only reader who can criticize such derivativeness is the one who has read widely enough and well enough to recognize the original model. Certainly if a given poem sounds like imitation T. S. Eliot, or imitation E. E. Cummings, or imitation Robert Frost, the poet deserves to be urged onto his own feet, and the reader who brings that criticism will be doing him a service, moving him toward his own distinctive voice, if he continues to write.

But on what basis can one dare to guess, or to hope, that a given student will continue to write after graduation and write well?

For twenty years I was some sort of writing coach attached to various university faculties. In common with my kind, and because the human ape is forever staring into a crystal ball in a confused hope of foreseeing the future, I made a regular occupational effort to outguess the time and to foresee which of my students would go on to achieve reputations as good writers. A gratifying number of them did, and their appearances in magazines and book lists was never a surprise. In the nature of the art, the good ones announce their promise.

Yet there were those who promised and were never again heard from. Some of them, as undergraduates, seemed at least as talented as their contemporaries who went on to establish themselves as good writers. There must be, one thinks retrospectively, clues to explain the failures of some and the successes of others. If there are such clues, they must also be clues to the nature of the writing process itself and to the writer's commitment to it.

An undergraduate tends, at best, to be an excited possibility. He is at the explorer's dawn of intellect and art. All is new and fresh, including his energy and history. And as a rule the world has not yet demanded him: he must meet his curricular requirements, but he has no bars to account to, no investment to worry about, no quota to meet, and usually no family to care for, no shoes to buy, no mortgage installments to meet. At any distance beyond graduation, those obligations may close in, or he himself may be used to the sad race and find himself scurrying down the rut in a career race of his own choosing that leaves him no time or desire for the fancifulness of sitting at paper to chase intangible foils into experienceable form until Joe Jones, who wrote, "My soul is boundless as the sea," is signing himself J. Damnick Jones and doing very well in the brassworks he started; Sue Smith, who, as Yeats cried out, "knew all Dante once," is bearing children to a dunce—or perhaps expanding her travel agency.

Make no mistake, it is possible to do other things well and still be a poet. Robert Frost was a shrewd dealer in real estate; Wallace Stevens was vice president of a major insurance company; William Carlos Williams was an actively practicing medical doctor. Come what may, a poet will write. A person needs time to tend to a mortal itch.

Writing is a stupid profession. There comes a time when every writer berates himself for sitting at a dull desk scrambling words on paper when he could be off building tangible worlds, making deals in the Waldorf, surf casting at Sandy Hook, or doing whatever one understands real life to be. What is it that draws the poet inevitably to the words and paper? What does he find there that is somehow more important than all other callings? What is it in the act of writing that possesses the writer?

There are probably as many answers as there are writers, yet to risk a single answer where many are possible, I will risk answering with Yeats, "Words alive are certain good." A writer is a person for whom words have flavors, shapes, sizes, moods, colors, presences, and ghosts. It is by the writing student's response to words that the good writing coach foresees a writer-to-be. All students feel the excitement of creativity. The word-sensitive has not only the excitement but the lure of the medium to fuel and force him when the first generic excitement of adolescence begins to wane.

W. H. Auden was once asked what advice he would give a young writer. He said that he would ask why the person wanted to write. If the young writer said, "Because I have something important to say," there would be nothing else to say. If the answer was "Because I like to hang around words and overhear them whispering to one another," there would be a great deal more to talk about, because the young person was responding to the one enduring lure.

In the line of my failures as a writing coach, I recall a young navy veteran I once hoped for. He had served on a tanker in the Pacific in World War II. For years he had stood his ocean watches; in an accumulation of boredom he had had time to think into a place inside himself. In his time off watch, he had read compulsively and widely and taken important influences into his style. At moments he could make his stinking, inescapable, wallowing tanker come alive as a true presence. He would sometimes lose the mood, but he would also find it again, sometimes memorably.

One of his stories was about a long search through the tail end of a typhoon for a courier in urgent need of refueling. He carried that story particularly well, his basic device being a relentless ticking off of the sort of ridiculous detail that makes the mind of the armed services even as the typhoon is scattering papers. And he brought it through well, concluding a bit limply, I thought, with, "We had finally arrived at our mid-ocean rendezvous."

In our conference on the story, I finally got around to "arrive." I would not insist, I told him, but I wanted to raise a question he must answer for himself. At what level did he mean to engage language? The English word "arrive," I pointed out, is simply a slightly charged way of pronouncing and spelling the Latin *ad ripa*, meaning "to the bank, or shore." Could one go "to the shore" in mid-ocean?

He shrugged, let me know he was no Latinist, and declared himself satisfied with "everyone's common understanding" that "to arrive" meant "to get there."

I tried one more instance. How would he feel about the usage "a crusading Egyptian politician"? He saw nothing wrong with that. I suggested that a crusade (from Latin *crux*) involved a motion toward the cross (Christian), and that any involvement an Egyptian might have with a crusade was likely to be on the other side of the action, and that to confuse the two sides could produce a comic confusion of history. He decided to be consistent and he shrugged again; everyone understood what was meant. The politician was a man undertaking a campaign to improve things, and why worry about ancient Latin roots. He was writing today.

But it is in the nature of writing, and of the commitment to good writing, that a writer is one to whom all of the word is important. The root of a word is part of the conversation it is having with the other words it whispers to. It is part of the ghost of a word. At the risk of being both overly simple and overly venturesome, I will claim that it is not subjects but those ghosts the poet writes to. Rhythms, sounds, the sort of muscular involvement required to announce the words, root meanings, the interplay of the evolved meaning (everyone's common understanding), and the root of the word are parts of that ghost.

There is not a word that is not so haunted. Look at one that my lamented student might well have used richly, had he cared for ghosts. The evolved meaning of "overwhelm" is "to leave at an emotional loss," to overpower or overcome. The old English root is *hwelm,* surviving in our word "helm," once signifying the rails of the ship, having moved back to the stern. The root image in "overwhelm" is of the sea crashing in over the side of an open (Viking) boat, coming in "over the hwelm," which is to say crashing over the tholes.

No one knows enough about words to chase all of them down, but every good writer knows a bit, will learn more, and would like to know all. T. S. Eliot knew about "overwhelm" and used it to masterful effect in "Prufrock." Early in the poem he leads the reader to "an overwhelming question." The real ghost of "inundation by the sea" becomes the first declaration of a theme. Bit by bit the theme of undersea imagery develops through the poem. It resolves itself underwater "in the chambers of the sea." The ghost of the word becomes part of the poem's essential structure.

There will always be the mystified student to whom such attention to words and such exquisite (Latin *exquirere,* to search out) usages are new and strange—did Eliot really mean to evoke the root image in that way? The answer is, simply, "Yes, and don't fight the idea but think about it until you grasp the possibilities of that quality of attention." In the sensate drift between the yammering ape of ego and the dreamself of idea, it is this quality of attention that may most nearly define us as human entities.

The mind may be, as Richard Wilbur says it is, like a bat beating about in a cave:

> Contriving by a kind of senseless wit
> Not to conclude against a wall of stone.

He concludes his poem ("Mind") with an idea no computer could respond to but that every human must:

> And has this simile a like perfection?
> The mind is like a bat. Precisely. Save
> That in the very happiest intellection
> A graceful error may correct the cave.

The quality of a poet's attention to words is always toward the possibility of that graceful error. If the physical world is indeed a wall that encloses us, our ghosts may yet melt through it to a perception fact will not come to. It is the echoing self of the inner mind that gives power to the writing.

Words and the ghosts of words are the key to that self. Sit down with no intent but to describe the room in which you find yourself at this instant. Let it be your sole purpose to make the room visible to a reader. Do not be fancy. Do not be important. Do not be significant. Be accurate and visual.

By the time you have written as much as a dozen sentences—if you are word-sensitive—the words you have chosen to describe light, space, shape, color, perspective, will have begun to exhale ghosts. Let's say there is an ancestral photo in the room, so you describe the ancestral faces as "swimming off through faded sepia to some place under the light." Fine—those old photos do fade, and we all know what sepia is. It is also the Latin name for the cuttlefish, which derives from a Greek verb meaning to make rotten (the ink of the squid was believed to rot things). You now have the ghost of an idea that was nowhere in your mind when you began writing.

What ghost is it? It is made of ancestral shadows, the faded light of old photos, of human faces reading into time, drowning in time, in the undersea squid-stain of time (which is of course the watery equivalent of the Greek nether-world, which is of course of time and death and the passage of light). What ghost of what idea is that?

It is what you know how to write about that was nowhere in your conscious mind when you began writing. It is the ghost of your writing, its word-awakened ghost, and the ending is not now between you and your starting intention but between you and its awakened ghost. That ghost is your encounter. The writing will be finished when you have laid the ghost to rest in some formal resolution.

That, I believe, is the process of writing a poem—working to awaken a ghost and lay it to rest. That process is not open to those who do not care about words. The good beginners care from the start; the good writers never stop caring. Writing is the act of caring. The writer bangs around words to overhear them whisper because that whisper is the writer's mortal attention awakened. Poetry has no other subject, and no other way of engaging itself.

There are many with a desire, even a passion, to write who are never able to live with the language in this way, for the desire to write poetry cannot of itself produce the ability: a talent is required, and that mortal itch to do, though it must be the consort of talent, is no substitute for it. Teachers and loyal fellow students should be wary of overencouraging student poets. Tremendous amounts of human energy have been expended wastefully by people who yearned to be poets but lacked the essential talent. In many cases those same people, had they not been overencouraged, might have learned to direct their energies in other directions better suited to their natural talents. And many of them might have come to happier lives.

For the chances, if only statistically, are overwhelmingly against the possibility that a student poet will become an accomplished poet, or even that he will still be writing five or ten years out of school. Any college or university is lucky if in the course of any twenty years, it graduates three people who will have a book of poems published except at their own expense. With great luck, one of those three may write some poems that will survive. No school has any expectation at any time of graduating a major poet. Robert Frost, had he graduated from Harvard, would have been about the class of '94. Wallace Stevens took his law degree in 1903. William Carlos Williams graduated in medicine from the University of Pennsylvania in 1906. All the colleges in the United States in the decade-and-more between 1894 and 1906 produced these three poets of major consequence and no others. And, at that, it was a rich decade.

So the question becomes: by what marks may one venture to identify that rare student who has what is required and could go on to greatness—or at least to produce work of real consequence?

Let me suggest that if the student is drawn to poetry by a self-feeding excitement over words, rhyme, the "feel" of a line, metaphor, image, the structure of a stanza, rhythm, the form of the whole poem—then poetry is to him a lively and immediate experience and one that can remain important through every change of mind and circumstance. Such a student is, in a sense, like a passionate chess-player: come fire, theft, collision, divorce, depreciation, or irreligion, he is going to sneak away from his surface concerns and lose himself in a game of chess, rubbing his hands as he sits down to the board.

In a deeper and more self-rewarding way, the true poet is like that chess-player, except that he does not escape from

his life to his passion, but joins the two in one act of per-
ceiving his life and bringing it to form in the poem. It is by
his way with those formal elements that one knows the
poet. And it is by the way the student poet begins to develop his own way with those formal elements that one is
justified in daring to hope for him.

That interest in the formal elements of poetry, needless
to say, is the antithesis of "self-expression." What does the
self-expresser care about formal elements? His concern is to
say, "Me, me, me: This is the way I feel!" So far as poetry
is concerned, he is wasting his time and should be told
so. The student, on the other hand, who will devote attention to the formal elements of poetry, though he may
never accomplish anything as a poet in his own right, is
learning how to read poetry. He is acquiring into his life
the great roll call of English poetry from Chaucer, through
Shakespeare and Donne, to Keats and beyond. No one ever
learned to read Keats by self-expressing in free verse.

So these are fair questions to ask: Does the writer seem to
have a sense of rhythm? Are his lines interesting rhyth-
mical units and do they unite into something like a self-
moving rhythm from beginning to end? Does he take on
the discipline of rhyme, and if he does, do the rhymes manage to fall into place with some sense of inevitability or does
the necessity to find rhyme force the writer to use an awkward, unidiomatic, or too-literary word or construction?
Bad rhyming is easy enough to demonstrate. It is either
hackneyed (God/sod; life/strife) or forces the poet to say
something very differently from how he would normally
have said it (if/a million years I should live/I would not ever
you forgive).

Such poetic elements as the quality of the individual
line, rhythmic units, and the structure and rhythm of the
total poem will not lend themselves to quick illustration.
Judgment in such matters must be based on wide and care-

ful reading. There is still the matter of the poet's words, however, and here the student poet can reasonably be his own critic. How well does the poet use words?

√ The student reader who wants to develop a critical perception will do well to forget about what the poem "means." He should read, rather, phrase by phrase. Read it aloud: Does it come well off the tongue? Think back to it: Does it stick in the mind? Look at it again: Is it sharp? How many words are being used to say how much? Could the same thing be said as richly in fewer words?

Look at the verbs. English has a treasury of verbs in every metal: tight, gnarled Anglo-Saxon verbs with the ring of iron to them; nicely minted historic verbs such as "to burke," "to boycott," and "to bowdlerize," neat as the king's shillings; good slangy and dialect verbs like new and used copper pennies, "to high-tail it," "to buy," and "to lay back"; strange coinages from every European language—all these and the big paper-money verbs from Latin and Greek. Does the poet seem to know anything about the domestic and international market in verbs? Is he a good collector, and does he arrange his collection in a way that makes it interesting in itself? Or is he just rattling along using the verbs anyone would have chosen, less than a dime's worth of all the wealth available to him.

Above all, the poet should scrutinize his adjective-noun combinations. How many of the adjectives actually provide some sensory intensification of the noun or at least help identify it? How many simply pass a judgment on it? The adjective-noun combination "beautiful sunset," for example, passes a judgment upon the noun "sunset"; it offers no clue to the beauty. By this time in history, it is all but impossible to modify "sunset" in a fresh and rich way, but either of the following would be an improvement over "beautiful"; "rayed sunset," "postcard sunset." These combinations make it possible for the reader to experience some specific element of the sunset instead of having to take the writer's word for it.

✓ As with the adjectives, so with the metaphors. Do the metaphors make for sensation and experience? "He looked hurt" is a pallid statement that might in the right context be sharpened into the simile: "His eyes fled like two dogs stoned." Is the poet able to bring his statement to that sort of like?

If teachers will look for such formal elements in poems, they may well teach themselves something about how to read a poem, and they may well be able to make criticisms that will help student poets to write better.

Serious Joy

Aᴄʟᴀssʀᴏᴏᴍ is not the ideal place for poetry. I wish we could take it up on a moun-
tain and shout it across from peak to peak, or take it out on
a picnic, or just take it into our lives. Poetry may be light;
it may be frivolous, and certainly a willing frivolity is part
of it; but it has to be passionate. The classroom has to be
rational. I am not suggesting that you should convert the
classroom into a scene of passion. There are enough difficulties in it. But it is necessary to remember that the material we are trying to deal with rationally in class is a playfully passionate experience.

Robert Frost spoke of a place "where love and need are
one, and the work is play for mortal stakes." That is the
kind of play I mean. If there is no play, nothing happens.
There is no seriousness without play.

Certainly no one need doubt the sincerity, the sobriety,
the strength of purpose of Mormon history, for example.
But the Tabernacle Choir does not sing sobriety and solem-

nity; they sing joy. That is what poetry deals with. Poetry is not moral nor immoral; it is before morality. It is like a heartbeat. If you are dedicated to bad ends, a good heart will help you function in an evil way. If you are dedicated to good ends, a good heart will help you function in a good way. It is only a resource.

I did some work in theology while I was translating Dante. I needed the background of it. I read quite a number of medieval disquisitions—very learned, very obtuse—on all sorts of subjects, including what makes the angels fly, and why they can fly; none of the medieval magicians got it down, but I think I know why. Angels can fly because they take themselves lightly. That is not established theology, but I suggest it as a better answer than I have found.

We have to have absence of play. Robert Frost also said, "A poem begins in delight and ends in wisdom." There is a kind of wisdom that cannot be approached except in the act of joy.

I was talking to some teachers once and found myself discussing a poem by Elizabeth Bishop, a poem called "The Fish." It's a long, skinny poem—the lines are short. It goes down the page in a thin way with a thin, very prosy rhythm. The way a poem looks on the page is important. That is part of the structure of the thing.

Well, I came to the part where she caught this fish in a pond. It was a huge fish, the monarch of the pond. It had six leaders broken off in its lower lip. It had outwitted any number of fishermen.

She caught this very wily fish and held it out of the water and was looking at it. Now, she did a kind of looking that I don't think many of us would be capable of. She said of the fish:

> I looked into his eyes
> which were far larger than mine

118

but shallower, and yellowed,
the irises backed and packed
with tarnished tinfoil
seen through the lenses
of old scratched isinglass.

Now just as a job of using our eyes, let us take that passage into our imaginations. I used to wish there were courses called elementary looking, intermediate looking, and advanced looking. In part, a writers' workshop is a course in how to use our eyes.

Now I have had students who could look at a fish and get the beginning of that description. They could get as good as, "I looked into his eyes." But then a good student could say, "which were far larger than mine, but shallower and yellowed." A good student could go that far. But I have never had a student who could write the next few words: "The irises backed and packed with tarnished tinfoil." The analogy is exact and the coloration is exact—the tarnished tinfoil.

She falls in love with the looking. Then the poem ends with, "And I let the fish go."

There is a sudden release of joy. That's an affirmation. You are not being preached to. It is like hearing a choir sing, "And I let the fish go." It is a praise; it praises the world. What is the world for but to be lived in and responded to? This is the best job I know of in English literature of looking at a fish's eye. What is so important about looking at a fish's eye? I think the first answer is that anything significantly looked at is significant.

But that is only a beginning, that is only an evasion, because what does "significant" mean? Putting it another way, a thing is significant that teaches us something about ourselves. Elizabeth Bishop teaches me with both a sense of delight and a sense of shame. She teaches me how well it is possible to see this world, and then she shames me that I haven't looked better, that I haven't entered my own act of joy sufficiently. She educates me. She makes me want to identify more closely. She enriches me in this way. I am glad for her, and it is a shudder of pleasure when she says, "And I let the fish go." I want to let all fish go in this way. It is an affirmation.

Beyond that, it is never the size of a thing looked at that counts but the size of the mind that is doing the looking. It takes intelligence to look, and this is a point the unfrivolous always lose. If we try to get too serious and too systematic about the arts, we lose this essential ingredient.

I recall my son one day coming home from the first grade. It was autumn and he had just learned a little ditty in school. It was obsessive, the way a tune can become obsessive. And he was having such a wonderful time. It ran:

> I rake the leaves
> Up in a hump,
> And then I bend
> My knees and jump.

He had jumped all the way home from school saying that, and he jumped into the house, and he jumped upstairs, and he jumped up into his room. His room was above the dining room where we had a large chandelier, and the chandelier kept going, so I had to go upstairs and kill his poetic impulse. But he was having a marvelous time. He was obsessed by this happy rhythm of, "I rake the leaves up in a hump, and then I bend my knees and jump." Try it on a first grader. See if he doesn't get an instant joy out of that sort of thing.

Just for the frivolous pleasure of poetry, if you like, there is a marvelous sonnet. It's by Witter Bynner, and it's one of my favorite tricks in poetry. It contains one word per line— nothing but the sonnet rhyme scheme. That is about as

thin as you can get with the sonnet. I have tried for years to
find another fourteen words that would perform this trick
well. No luck. It's called "An Aeronaut to His Love," and
it goes like this:

> I
> Through
> Blue
> Sky
> Fly
> To
> You.
> Why?
> Sweet
> Love,
> Feet
> Move
> So
> Slow.

That's all there was to it. But look, in the fourteen words
he has observed the a-b-b-a, a-b-b-a, c-d, c-d, e-e rhyme
scheme. The first eight lines ask a question; the next six
lines answer it. That is the octet and the sestet. It divides
properly, and the tone of it is the tone of the sonnet. That
is a tremendous lot to get into fourteen words: "I through
blue sky fly to you. Why? Sweet love, feet move so slow."
What we would have lost is the frivolity.

Here is an exercise in pure poetry. I was once looking up
the word "widgeon." I had known the word for a long time,
but I could not point to any specific duck and say, "That is
a widgeon." I looked at the roots, as I like to do, and
couldn't figure out what it had come from. I ran it down to
Latin, *ardea*, for heron, which is a long way off.

But I had the word "widgeon" in mind, and as I was looking at the page, I saw another word, "wicopy." That turned

out to be a word derived from the Algonquin Indians, the name of a particular tree. So when I tried to run down the tree, it said, some sort of broadleafed trees, a specimen of which is *Tilia glabra.*

In all this inquiry—you see how scholarly one gets—I found myself saying, "A widgeon in a wicopy—a widgeon in a wicopy." It wants to syncopate, doesn't it? But I'm not going to let you accuse me of being stupid. The writer has to pretend to be smarter than the reader. I know that ducks don't roost in trees, so that gave me a second line: "A widgeon in a wicopy, in which no widgeon ought to be." But I gathered myself, and now I obviously needed to go for "w's"; what came up was "a widowed widgeon was." "Widowed," I thought, was a good choice. It has a sounded and a muted "w," so I had a pattern: "A widgeon in a wicopy in which no widgeon ought to be, a widowed widgeon was." I liked the way it syncopated.

The joy was in seeing if I could repeat the pattern without stumbling, and the word that came to me was the key word for the next pattern, "wickiup." You know what a wickiup is. You take willow branches or something and make your frame; it's boy scout work. So I began, "While in a willow wickiup"—that gave me a lot of "w's." Now I needed a "w" Indian to keep this going, and I settled on "Wichita." But I wasn't sure Wichita was a word for a tribe or for a river or for an area. I looked that up in the dictionary, and it said Wichita was indeed an Indian tribe, so I was safe: "While in a willow wickiup, a Wichita sat down to sup with other Wichitas."

Here is something you do in poetry. I had said, "a widowed widgeon." If you widow a widgeon in a poem, you have to explain why—you have to account for it. It's like a theme in music. Once you have introduced it, you have to answer it. That's the fun of the performance. I got myself

into trouble and I came out with what I submit is an exercise in logic. The whole thing goes:

> A widgeon in a wicopy,
> In which no widgeon ought to be,
> A widowed widgeon was.
> While in a willow wickiup,
> A Wichita sat down to sup
> With other Wichitas,
> And what they whittled as they ate
> Included what had been of late
> A widgeon's wing.

But that isn't finished. It hasn't rhymed yet:

> . . . While in a willow wickiup,
> A Wichita sat down to sup
> With other Wichitas,
> And what they whittled as they ate
> Included what had been of late
> A widgeon's wing.
> 'Twas thus, the widgeon in the wicopy,
> In which no widgeon ought to be,
> A widowed widgeon was.

It seals itself. Poetry cannot save souls, but in case one's
number does come up, mightn't it improve the conversation in heaven?

Teaching Poetry

THE school system annually receives into its beginning classes an audience that over-flows with the joy and immediacy of poetry. The same system annually graduates from its high schools a horde of adolescents who, with rare exceptions, are either wary of poetry or hostile to it. In trying to fix the cause for this strange change from the sense of delight to which all healthy children are born, one might point the finger at the home, at the church, at television, or at the culture in general. In each case, the finger would have something to point to. Certainly the school system cannot be expected to accomplish by itself a kind of education society wants, yet some part of the decay of poetic pleasure between grade one and grade twelve must be chargeable to the schools. Poetry, in the high schools, is almost always badly taught.

There can be no rescue from the thinly taught course in poetry. The minimum requirement for the teacher is a human mind. Obviously we can build classrooms faster than we can educate such teachers to fill them. The constantly increasing number of classrooms can only mean that many of them must be staffed by clerks. Clerks do reasonably well with simple materials involved in such courses as typing, and the elementary levels of such courses as physics, biology, and chemistry. But they will do badly in history and English. And inevitably they will do their clerical worst in dealing with poetry.

They will do badly because the essential language of any art form is multiple. To experience that language, one must think more than one thought at a time. The multiplicity of the simultaneity are inseparable, as in a pun. It simply will not do to get one side of a pun now, another next Tuesday, yet a third on the Fourth of July. The good reader of poetry must develop that native suppleness and fluency of mind that is inseparable from the humanities and which is basically the ability to receive a two- or three-headed thought in an instant.

Consider that the entire curriculum is made up of two basic sorts of courses. In one sort it is possible to teach nothing but answers. In the other sort, answers are all but irrelevant: there are only questions. Therein lies the real distinction between training and education. Any course that can be taught with the answers already set is a training course and, therefore, preliminary to education. Clerks must, of course, be trained, and so trained they do well enough with answer-courses. But to teach questions requires a teacher, and teachers must be not trained but educated.

Many of the disciplines that begin as training do, of course, develop into education. When a student begins high school physics, he deals in simple, specific questions with firm answers, and he learns the method of extracting those answers. But if that student goes on in physics, he will have begun to run out of answers in college, and he will

certainly have run out of them by the time he is in graduate
school. He will have begun to explore the unknown. For
that, he must learn how to ask his questions and must often
settle for partial or ambiguous answers. He will have learned,
in fact, that what he does leads more readily to new questions than to answers. He is then—and only then—an
educated physicist. Which is to say that he has begun the
endless speculative process into the unknown.

The difference between the sciences and the humanities
is fixed in the fact that the students in the humanities must
plunge almost at once into the sort of intellectual speculation and uncertainty that the science student can delay
until much later in his career.

The speculation of the humanities involves the student
in his ideas of value, in his emotions, in his ability to per-
ceive, and in his vicarious projection into all sorts of aesthetic and historical experiences. The humanities question
and remake life itself. Only a teacher of intellectual and of
emotional depth can be a good guide to the experience of
the humanities.

The school system cannot put into its English classrooms
teachers of this humanely educated order for the simple reason that there are not enough of them to go round. Let the
point be made without rancor. The rewards offered by a career in teaching are no overwhelming lure. The school system must recruit what it can get. Praise be to the good
ones. The fact remains the most of the work must be done
by clerks who lack real grasp of their material.

My last experience with teaching teachers was at Rutgers
in 1960–61 when I gave a Saturday morning course for
teachers in Poetic Method, a graduate course for high school
teachers working toward an M.A. I had, I believe, twenty-
seven students enrolled. On the first day of class I outlined
what was essentially an easy graduate course. Certainly I required less of my teachers than I should have required of a

comparable body of graduate students in English; much less. I outlined the required reading for the course—less than half of what I would have demanded of regular graduate students—and I asked for two minor papers and one major paper in each semester. By the next Saturday my enrollment had fallen to nineteen, simply after the description of the course. I finished the year with eleven students. At least I am prepared to certify that there are eleven teachers in the New Jersey high school system who have demonstrated a basic grasp of the methods of teaching poetry. But I must also add that of those who enrolled for the course on description, sixteen fled apparently in something like terror, from the opening description of what was a seriously relaxed graduate course.

The quality of the teachers generally drawn to the profession of English is only the first problem. Had schools of education been able to recruit superior talent for future teachers of English, they must still stand charged with having failed to train them for the vital and resonant teaching of poetry. And for this failure, the English departments must stand equally charged.

Poetry is basically compounded of diction, image or metaphor, rhythm, and form. It is remarkable above all for the fact that it carries with it an implicit notation that dictates the rate at which it shall be read. It scores what is to be emphasized and what is to be subordinated. It slows the voice at one point and hurries it over another. It declares its silences as clearly as does a music score, and it hangs the structure of the poem—which is to say the poem's emotional weight—on those silences. To be sure, that notation is not as visible as the notation of music, but it is there, and one who lacks a sense of it, lacks the sense of poetry.

So our colleges generally share the failure of the schools of education in tending to teach everything about a poem except its poetry. Graduate students have labored endlessly at source work, the history of ideas, biography, textual matters, comparative literature (usually as a branch of the history of ideas), archive combing, historical background, and seventy-seven kinds of special analysis ranging from psychiatry to semantics, but not one in a hundred knows about a poem what any graduate of, say, the Juilliard School, knows about a piece of music.

Most graduate students can make some sort of stab at answering questions about such matters as I have listed above. But ask a question about the notation of poetry and almost invariably the student does not know where to begin.

"There are various theories of metrics," one may say. "Within your own theory, do you think it is possible for a caesura to occur within a metric foot, or must it always fall between metric feet?"

I have asked that sort of question of many graduate students. I have yet to find one who can come up with the beginnings of a speculation about it.

Certainly that is not the sort of question, nor the level of discussion, that a teacher is likely to find appropriate to public school teaching. I insist, however, that it is the sort of question—along with many more such—that the teacher must have asked himself.

Is it possible to say that a teacher lacks real training in the nature of poetry because the schools of education have only the vaguest sense of the nature of poetry, and because the departments of English have tended to study everything about poetry except the poem itself?

The Poem as a Made Thing

I USED to blame the schools of education for the failure of poetry in our school system. I don't any longer. I have found many a school of education all but pathetically eager to experiment, but the direction of the experimentation has to come from the English departments, and the English departments are too busy turning out historians, social workers, structural linguisticians, historians of ideas, biographical critics, and textual critics. All of these are valuable disciplines, but I don't think a historian should be turned loose on aesthetics. Too few teachers are prepared to teach the poem as a made thing.

As with music, I want to think of a poem as a self-entering, self-generating, self-sealing form. It arises in response to itself, but all sorts of things tempt teachers to a surface treatment of it. They can read a poem, have it discussed, and then have a weekly theme to assign. It is easy to say, "Write a theme on the meaning of this poem" as if it were a sermon text. The poem is something else; it is not a meaning.

131

The best way to look at a poem would be to spend many, many hours with a blackboard and pieces of paper, to chart the structure of the poem, speak an hour about the poem, then come back another hour and speak about that poem, to show how it is put together, how its words choose one another, how its rhythms choose one another, how its forms choose one another. But we can't do that. We should spend a month doing nothing but talking about one poem per hour to get some data, some detail, and then begin to generalize.

Here is a poem by Richard Eberhart on what might strike one as a non-poetic subject. It's called "The Cancer Cells." Eberhart looked through a microscope and saw these sinister shapes, sinister and repulsive and yet attractive. We all know the attraction of the repulsive; it's one of the things art has played with as a subject.

> Today I saw a picture of the cancer cells,
> Sinister shapes with menacing attitudes.
> They had outgrown their test-tube and advanced,
> Sinister shapes with menacing attitudes,
> Into a world beyond, a virulent laughing gang.
> They looked like art itself, like the artist's mind,
> Powerful shaker, and the taker of new forms.
> Some are revulsed to see these spiky shapes;
> It is the world of the future too come to.
> Nothing could be more vivid than their language,
> Lethal, sparkling and irregular stars,
> The murderous design of the universe,
> The hectic dance of the passionate cancer cells.
> O just phenomena to the calculating eye,
> Originals of imagination. I flew
> With them in a piled exuberance of time,
> My own malignance in their racy, beautiful gestures
> Quick and lean: and in their riot too

I saw the stance of the artist's make,
The fixed form in the massive fluxion.

I think Leonardo would have in his disinterest
Enjoyed them precisely with a sharp pencil.

There is some rather loose stuff in the beginning, but note how the last two lines are thrust against the first passage. That is the essence of the poem. I want to argue that a poem consists of one thing thrust against another across a silence. It is like music, in that you set up a passage, you pause, and against it you push a counter passage. That is not a statement; that is an experience, a shape, a thing made. It is like a statue, like a painting. From that you can, of course, extract all sorts of things. Those two last lines win from me something like total admiration. There is a sense of horror at the cancer cell, then the silence, and in another tone of voice, "I think Leonardo would have in his disinterest enjoyed them precisely with a sharp pencil."

I would have no objection to turning a class loose on what it means "to enjoy precisely with a sharp pencil." I don't think the class would be ready for it, but let them try something they are not ready for. I'm tired of having students do things they are ready for.

That is a hard concept to get, "to enjoy precisely with a sharp pencil." It is so easy to be loosely beautiful, but "Leonardo enjoyed precisely with a sharp pencil" is a concept. You may ask, "What is the artist's disinterest?" What *is* the disinterest of the arts? And, a counter question would be, "In what way are they passionate and partisan?"

I have no objection to chipping off pieces of poems and making theme discussions of them, so long as it's understood that those theme discussions are not about the essence of the poem, though they move around it. Poetry is an impure art. Though it forever becomes involved in ideas, and contains them, it continually resists them.

I will argue that it is not necessary for a poem to mean anything outside itself. If the poem means itself hard enough, it will achieve meaning. Some of the most sublime statements about the human position on this planet have been made by poets, but they have been made by those poets who are most immediately involved in the handling of their own musicality. I have never heard an orchestra conductor say to the musicians in rehearsal, "You are not being beautiful enough. You are not being universal enough. You are not being awe-stricken enough." He says, "Let's take it five measures before the key change; pick up the tempo; someone's blowing flat."

If what you are working for is beauty, that is the language you have to speak. I don't know how many people have had their minds entrapped in a kind of vacuity by an ill-chosen interpretation of Keats' "Ode on a Grecian Urn." "Beauty is truth, truth beauty, that is all ye know on earth and all ye need to know." Beauty and truth are no irrelevancies, but they can exist only as they are exemplified in a specific and managed work of art. You cannot say, "Give me three yards of beauty. Give me a bushel of truth." Beauty has to be captured in something. It has to be in-formed, put into a form, and that form is a matter of specification and of management.

Form is order. Outside of this is chaos. The human mind has a deep need for order. Art is a way of ordering the world. Robert Frost said once: "A poem is a momentary stay against confusion. You can't get clarified to stay so. Let you not think that."

You get a glimpse of form and order and it is an assurance, a gift, a happiness, a shape, and a firm place. Then the wind blows, and you are off again but with a renewed sense of possibility, because there has been a glimpse of form. Frost said, even of a smoke ring, that it is good to see

there for that instant before it dissolves.
ist to see it shaped and ordered.
ergetic, young psyches come into the
e with poetry, loving it, knowing exactly
owing how to take very difficult poems.

isty, moisty morning
loudy was the weather,
I chanced upon an old man
Clad all in leather.
He began to compliment
And I began to grin,
How do you do? How do you do?
And how do you do again?

I suppose Freudians could go to work on that wet leather
and the mistiness of the morning as maybe amniotic. I am
not at all sure but what they could make some sense of the
subterranean and the unconscious dance of symbols. On
the other hand, my daughter at two knew exactly what that
poem meant. It meant that when you got to the last line
you bowed three times and then giggled. This is a lovely
meaning. I would like to write a poem that would have
little girls bowing to the east, bowing to the west, and bowing to the one they love best and then giggling. That is
meaning enough.

(I have gotten into trouble with some of my colleagues by
insisting that not only was Lewis Carroll a better poet than
Wordsworth but a more profound intellect. He didn't ser-
monize, he didn't come out with academic terms, but he
had a basic, palpable understanding of the depths of the
psyche. The things happening in *Alice* are more profoundly
intellectual than the things expounded in Wordsworth.)

But what causes the loss of a child's immediacy? By the
time they get to high school most are certainly dead in the

head where poetry is concerned. Some of it must have to do with teaching. Many teachers will get too reverent and too awe-stricken in front of the poem or transmit a sense of unreality. I used to hear "Class, isn't that beautiful?" That was the end of the discussion. It was not much to take home.

I don't think it is possible to teach anything until the teacher has elicited some enthusiasm. That is where teaching begins. As far as poetry is concerned, the job is not simple, but it reduces to one thing. Somehow the student has to be led to read a poem, to put it down, and to say "Wow!" From that point on he is teachable, but until that excitement has been elicited, until that response has been there, no teaching is possible. You may train, you may discipline, you may cause poems to be memorized by unexcited people, but only the excited can learn.

So the kind of examination question I would like to see is not, "What does this poem mean?" but, "What words in the poem spring from the word which is circled in line 1?" That is expectation and answer. A word calls another word into being; it has a certain flavor. You select words whose flavor matches that of the first. The teacher may circle one word in line five of a twelve-line poem and say, "Circle all of the words in the poem related to this one." If they circle them right they are responding to the poetry. They realize what choices are being made. It is possible to develop meaningful, useful criteria for diction, for image or metaphor, for rhythm, and for form. Once these criteria have been established, once a student can recognize the difference between a soft diction and a hard diction; an Anglo-Saxon diction and a Latinate diction; a loose diction and a tight one; a smooth-going diction and a crabbed one; he can begin to make comparisons and to evaluate.

There is no reason to be afraid to talk about the meters of poetry. I was in navigation school during the war, and we had to learn Morse code. If you add in the numbers, there are thirty-six "metric feet" you have to learn before you can work a telegraph key. The boys just ate it up. They had no trouble getting Morse code. Boy Scouts learn it. You don't have to learn any code nearly that intricate in order to work out the metrics of poetry. All you really need is an iamb, a trochee, an anapest, a dactyl, a monosyllabic foot, a spondaic foot, and maybe an amphibrach tossed in. Seven or eight feet will give you all the basic measure you need to get the metrics of English poetry, and that isn't complicated. We used to learn it by a dance. *Dah* dit dit *dah dah*—Shave and a haircut. It is not difficult.

The best example I know of a poet simply enjoying words in order to overhear them whispering to one another occurs in the worksheets of "The Eve of St. Agnes," one of the triumphs of the nineteenth century by John Keats. The poem is about a Romeo and Juliet situation in which Porphyro loves Madeline, but their families are feuding. There are two sub-plots. If on the Eve of St. Agnes a girl performs a certain ritual, which includes never looking behind her, she will dream of her own true love forever. Then Angela, the aged *belle dame*, has smuggled Porphyro into Madeline's chamber, and he waits there for her to come from the feast in the castle below so they may elope that night.

While Porphyro is hiding in the closet, Madeline enters and begins to undress. This is rather precarious material for Keats. You can imagine how Homer might have treated this or Boccacio or Chaucer. All the details might be the same, but the tone would be different. Tone is one of the things you cannot paraphrase. It is very difficult to catch it; it has to go in answer to itself. Keats had to keep a certain air to the passage which was set in advance.

Madeline enters all dressed in white. There are stained-glass windows in her chamber, and the moon is full and bright as it can be only in poetry. It comes through the stained-glass window splotching light on her white dress so that she looked like a stained-glass saint. You are not responding to the poetry unless you respond to the particular joy Keats had in enumerating and saying the names of the colors. His joy in handling these splotches of colors, the joy of saying "amethyst," and the sensuality of loving the words and their concepts was part of his diction. It sets up what happens in the next paragraph, for Porphyro is about to swoon with romantic delight, but she arises and anon his heart revives.

Maybe that is a poetic strategy because Keats wants to keep this scene from being fleshy. Maybe if the boy is about to swoon, he is less dangerous and more abstracted. This is already the third draft of this stanza. The worksheets are in the Houghton Library at Harvard, and you can see all his scratchings on it. His problem is to get Madeline undressed, but to keep the particular flavor of the music.

> Anon his heart revived: Her vespers done
> Of all its wreathed pearls she freed her hair,
> Unclasps her warmed jewels one by one . . .

The jewels are warmed because they have been in contact with her body. It is at that one remove that Keats wants to suggest her body. Note that we have "wreathed pearls," "warmed jewels." One follows from the other: adjective, noun; adjective, noun. It is like a chord sequence in music.

> Unclasps her warmed jewels one by one
> Loosens her bursting bodice . . .

Keats stopped right there. Bursting is obviously the wrong word. What sort of sequence is "wreathed pearls," "warmed jewels," "bursting bodice?" I know of no law that says Madeline could not be as buxom as she pleased and still have all the qualities that Keats wants. It is the flavor of the word that is wrong. It is the wrong tonality. It might have suited the Wife of Bath, but there is something excessive about bursting in this context that lacks the flavor and delicacy of wreathed and warmed.

Keats scratched it off, and then he tried to cheat. Poets are always trying to cheat. The good ones are resisting, and the bad ones go on cheating. They take the easy choices. A work of art is essentially a chain of choices. What measures the integrity, the morality, the values of the writer is the level on which the choices of a given poem are made. A poet can always put in something to fill out the line.

The minimum requirement for a good poem is a miracle. By a miracle I mean a better choice than anyone could have foreseen, including the writer. He gets himself into more trouble than he knows how to handle and then dances out of it.

Keats wrote "Loosens her bodice lace-strings." Aside from the fact that lace-strings stops the flow of the words, it is like a German noun. It is not really an adjective-noun combination. It doesn't follow: wreathed pearls, warmed jewels, bodice lace-strings. I could have crept up behind John Keats and said, "Nobody will notice if you put in bodice lace-strings; they will still like the poem. You can get away with it." Perhaps something of that thought had touched his mind, but he knew it was not good enough. He rejected it. He kept on trying all sorts of things. He scratched and scratched. That is the labor of it. He labored, until finally he came up with the right choices.

> Of all its wreathed pearls she frees her hair;
> Unclasps her warmed jewels one by one;
> Loosens her fragrant bodice.

"Fragrant" is certainly a customary enough and easy word. The poet is not straining for the fresh, unusual word. Sometimes, yes, but there is much more to be said for the fresh, usual word.

Why is "fragrant" right? "Wreathed pearls," "warmed jewels," "fragrant bodice." The bodice is "fragrant" because it has been touching her body, just as the jewels were warmed. In this context only, "fragrant" does for bodice exactly what "warmed" does for jewels. Therefore the two words are instantly related; it is as if you were stringing prose together.

If you had a whole binful of prose called the English Language, and you wanted to pick out a string of perfectly matched words, wouldn't these two belong side by side on the string? They are equal in size, in luster, in color, in suggestion, in all the qualities you want in a pearl. Warmed and fragrant are this closely akin for nonintellectual, felt, perceived, and sensory reasons, not for paraphrasable, rational, dictionary meanings. In poetry, the words choose each other. This is one way to talk about diction.

I don't begin to know the meaning of Shakespeare's "The Phoenix and the Turtle." It is a mysterious dark green, but I like to put it through my head. I don't know where it is going, but it makes lovely echoes as it goes, and the echoes have the sound of my name in them. I can't identify them, but I know it is a voice I want to speak to and hear. I would rather be confused by Shakespeare than clarified by my broker. To be a human being is to be confused. There are small confusions, and there are confusions the size of life, like listening to the sound of the sea at night, but if you want to clarify the sound of the sea at night, you cannot do it, you have to live into it.

Blake's "Tyger, Tyger, burning bright," can't be paraphrased. There is always language left over. We could talk about "Kubla Khan" as a visited place in the imagination of the English-speaking people. You have been there; I have been there. We could talk about it as we might talk about a visit to the Taj Mahal.

Think again of a poem as one thing thrusting against another across a silence. That is form. If you have developed criteria for diction, for metaphor, for rhythm, then as soon as you find the silence in a poem, you will find that at least one, usually two, and sometimes three of these elements have changed across the silence. That is all you need to know in order to unravel a poem in terms of itself. The diction will have changed from one side of the silence to the other, or the rhythm, or the metaphoric structure will have changed. This could be illustrated by an endless number of poems, but let me offer a very simple example.

> O western wind when wilt thou blow
> That the small rain down may rain?
> Christ, that my love were in my arms
> And I in my bed again.

That is a surviving fifteenth-century ballad fragment. To say the first two lines does not make a poem, and it is no poem to say the second two lines. It is a poem if you say the first two lines, pause, and then say against them the next two lines.

If poetry is taught in these terms, if we can develop some criteria for the kinds of diction (including rhyme), the kinds of rhythm, the kinds of metaphor, and the total pattern, and get students to identify them from one side of the poem to the other, we don't have to ask what a poem means. We are talking not about editorials or sermons but about poetry when we talk about diction, image or metaphor, rhythm, and form. Then we discover that we are talking about the things that make our emotions happen. We are talking about our lives in their immediate rather than their abstract terms. We are talking about a poem.

A NOTE ABOUT THE AUTHOR

THE only son of Italian immigrants, John Ciardi graduated magna cum laude from Tufts University in 1938 and received his M.A. in English literature from the University of Michigan the following year. A dominant presence on the American literary scene, John Ciardi served at various times as a professor of English at Harvard, the University of Missouri at Kansas City, and Rutgers; director of the Bread Loaf Writers Conference, host of the CBS magazine show "Accent," poetry editor of *Saturday Review,* translator of *The Divine Comedy,* and as a joyously irreverent lexicographer in his Browser's Dictionaries. He died on Easter Sunday, 1986.